The Book of Literar

D0547069

Other Books by Lewis Turco

A Book of Fears (Italian translations by Joseph Alessia), 1998

Shaking the Family Tree: A Remembrance, 1998

Bordello: A Portfolio of Poemprints, with George O'Connell, 1996

Emily Dickinson: Woman of Letters, 1993

The Public Poet, 1991

The Shifting Web: New and Selected Poems, 1989

Dialogue, 1989

The Fog: A Chamber Opera in One Act, with Walter Hekster, 1987

The New Book of Forms, 1986

Visions and Revisions of American Poetry, 1986

The Compleat Melancholick, 1985

American Still Lifes, 1981

Poetry: An Introduction through Writing, 1973

Pocoangelini: A Fantography & Other Poems, 1971

The Inhabitant, 1970

Awaken, Bells Falling: Poems 1959–1967, 1968

The Book of Forms: A Handbook of Poetics, 1968

First Poems, 1960

Lewis Turco

THE BOOK OF LITERARY TERMS

The Genres of Fiction, Drama,
Nonfiction, Literary Criticism,
and Scholarship

University Press of New England
Hanover and London

University Press of New England, Hanover, NH 03755
© 1999 by Lewis Turco
All rights reserved
Printed in the United States of America   5 4 3 2 1
CIP data appear at the end of the book

This book is dedicated to

JEAN

whose idea it was in the first place

Contents

Preface

The Book of Literary Terms, with its companion volume, *The Book of Forms: A Handbook of Poetics*, has been designed to be the most comprehensive guide of its kind available. It may be used as a personal reference or as a text and literary guide in virtually every course in the English curriculum. However, it is something more than simply an alphabetical listing of terms. It is organized in seven sections, the first of which is titled "Introduction to the Discipline of Literature"; this chapter is followed by "The Genres of Fiction," "The Genres of Drama," "The Genres of Nonfiction," and "The Genres of Literary Criticism and Scholarship."

Each of these chapters consists of brief essays covering various topics having to do with the overall subject under discussion. For instance, "Introduction to the Discipline of Literature" includes essays having to do with definitions of form, the word, syntax, genre, diction and style, and literary movements. Each of these essays contains illustrations of the terms discussed. At the end of each section will be found a "Chapter Glossary" containing terms that have not been covered in the essay or fuller discussions of some terms that were mentioned in passing. Thus, the book may be used not merely as a reference work in all literary contexts but also as a textbook in one genre or in several.

For instance, if one were working in the genre of fiction and wished to look up "character" or "characterization," one would turn directly to the chapter titled "The Genres of Fiction" and check through the chapter for subheadings that apply. One might also turn to the chapter glossary and look up the term in question. If one wished to find wider applications of the term, one would turn to the index at the back of the book to look up the term and find the numbers of all the pages where that term appears in the book. Or one might wish to begin directly with the index.

Another plan might be simply to begin reading the chapter or the essay containing the term in question. Nearby one would discover other basic elements of the short story, such as "plot," "atmosphere," and "theme" and such terms as "narrative voice," "rising action," "denouement," and so forth, all arranged in such a way as to lead the reader through the elements of the short story. Such a layout and plan make the book livelier and more interesting to read than an ordinary handbook.

The index is comprehensive; it will usually indicate that a particular term is to be found in more than one place in the body of the volume. For instance, many of the elements of fiction are also the elements of drama, and in looking up these references the reader will discover not merely similarities between terms used in fiction and drama but the differences as well. "Narrative voice" or "dramatic irony" would mean similar but somewhat different things in each of the genres.

It is the belief of the author that this volume is both comprehensive and comprehensible and that those who consult it will find it both usable and enjoyable to read. The one genre of literature that is not covered by this text is poetry, and that genre is covered by the companion volume, *The Book of Forms: A Handbook of Poetics*, 3rd edition (University Press of New England, 2000).

The Book of Literary Terms

Introduction to the Discipline of Literature

Form

Every element of language is a form of some kind. The *letters* of the *alphabet* are forms, *conventions* upon which the members of a culture have agreed in order to communicate; so are *words*, *phrases*, *clauses*, and *sentences*, whether spoken or written. *Phonemes* are the elemental bits of sound, like the *sonic units*—represented by the letters of the *alphabet*, including the *vowels* (**a**, **e**, **i**, **o**, **u**) and the *consonants* (all the rest of the letters)—that make up *morphemes*, which are the smallest language units that carry meaning, such as a single-*syllable word* like **a** or **it**, or a *prefix* like **pro-** as in "**pro**portion" or a *suffix* like **-ing** as in "walk**ing**." An *allophone* is a standard variation of a phoneme, such as the variations of the vowel **u** in b**u**t and m**u**te—see *consonance*. *Words*, which are the basic spoken or written *signifiers* (*units of signification*) of people who speak a *language*, are composed of various kinds of *sounds*, including *liquid* (like **el** and **ar**), *voiced* (like **ar**, **dee** and the *runic* **thorn** þ sound in **th**at); *plosive* (like **pee** and **dee**), *sibilant* (like **ess** and **zee**); *guttural* (like **kay** and **gee**); *open* (like the vowel sound in th**aw**; *closed* (like **ee**); *unvoiced* (like **ess**, **tee**, **kay**, and the thorn þ sound in **th**aw); and *continuant* (like **ell**, **em**, and **ng**). A *diphthong* is a gliding sound between two contiguous vowels (as in **ae**rie, c**oo**peration, l**eo**nine).

The Word

The science of language is *linguistics,* which studies the attributes and composition of human verbal communication; the *morphology,* or form and structure, of the words of a language, including *etymology,* their historical origins and derivations; *phonology,* inflections; *semantics,* meanings; *transformations,* shifts in morphology and semantics; and the formation of *compounds:* words made up of two or more individual words, such as **backyard**, **highboy**, and **nestegg**, or of the combination of transformed elements of words, as in *philology,* the love of language or of words, from the Greek "philo," meaning "loving," and "logos," meaning "learning" or "words."

Semiotics is the study of the *signs* used in communication. According to Roland Barthes, all signs may be subsumed under five *codes* or *rubrics: hermeneutic, semic, symbolic* (see these terms elsewhere in these pages), *proaireitic* (having to do with actions), and *cultural* (referring to a body of lore or a field of inquiry). *Stylistics* is a branch of linguistics, the study of the use of constituents of language, such as *tropes*—figures of speech, including descriptions, similes, and metaphors—in specific contexts. The origins and history of proper names is *onomastics.*

Etymology, as was mentioned above, is the study of words and their historical origins, relationships with words in other languages, and alterations in *morphology*—form and meaning. An *etymon* (plural *etymons* or *etyma*) is a *root word* in a language that serves as the basis for words in other languages or as the original word form in a later version of the same language; or it may be a morpheme that serves as the basis for *derivatives* (i.e., words that are derived from some source) and *compounds* (i.e., words that are made up from combinations of two or more sources). Each word is an *aural*—heard, or *indited*—written sign that stands for something else. An agreement on the meaning of a word or other language unit is a *definition.* For example, if one were to say to someone else, "I blygle your mordalpot," the other person might say, "What are you talking about?"

"Well, where I come from **blygle** means 'a strong feeling of admiration and caring,' and **mordalpot** means 'the filaments that grow on one's head.'"

"Oh, you mean you love my hair! Thank you. Your hairdo is nice too."

Verbs (like **blygle**) are words that signify actions: **run, jump, laugh, handle, kiss**, for example. *Nouns* (like **mordalpot**) are *substantives*, either *concrete nouns* that stand for objects, such as **table, brick, shoe,** or **roadway**, or *abstract nouns* that stand for thoughts and ideas, such as **God, love, soul, honor, happiness**. Basically, concrete nouns may be conventionally defined, whereas abstract nouns cannot be, for no two people will agree absolutely on definitions for any of these words. Many abstract nouns, such as these last mentioned, and some concrete nouns, such as **flag** and **apple pie,** are *cues*, words that elicit conditioned responses, as an actor is conditioned to respond to a spoken cue in a *play*. An *adjective* is a word or phrase that modifies a noun, generally by preceding it: **pretty** baby, **blue** sky; an *adverb* modifies a verb (ran **slowly**, ate **carefully**), an adjective (a **wonderfully** pretty baby), or another adverb (ran **extremely** slowly).

An *archaism* is an obsolete word, one that no longer appears in the average *lexicon*—that is, *dictionary* or list of words—of a language. For instance, the word "chirming" once meant the sound that birds make when they flock in the trees in the fall preparatory to migration. The English language no longer has a current word for such a phenomenon.

A *colloquialism* is a word or phrase used in ordinary conversation that is not considered to be in good enough taste or at a high enough level of diction to be used in polite conversation or in literary writing. It lies between *slang* and *formal speech*—see *levels of diction*. *Cacozelia* denotes the use of neologisms, which are *nonce words* minted for particular occasions or situations, as, for instance, the terms "hip" and its *variant* "hep" (as in the 1940s jazz slang term "hepcat" and perhaps derived from the *etymon* "hipi" or "hepi" from the Wolof language of West Senegal, meaning "to be aware of") were once American slang neologisms meaning "in the know," particularly about jazz. Later, in the 1960s, the neologism "hippy" was coined to mean someone who was a free spirit or "bohemian," with ties to the drug scene. Later still, the term developed into the neologism "Yippy," at least partially an *acronym* meaning a member of the **Y**outh **I**nternational **P**arty. When the fun-filled days of the Vietnamese "police action," a *euphemism*, were long over, a further derivation was invented: "yuppy," another acronym standing for "**y**oung, **u**pwardly-mobile **p**rofessional **p**erson." Actually, it should have been "yump-y," but the coiner or coiners evidently wanted the *overtone* (*secondary definition*) of "yes-men" to be implied by the slang term "yup."

A *coinage* is a *neologism* invented by a known author, as, for instance, the word "ent" coined by J. R. R. Tolkien in his *trilogy* (three-novel *cycle*), *The Lord of the Rings*. (Tolkien actually invented an entire language for these books, "Elvish," spoken by the elves who were characters therein.) An "ent" is a "tree-being" or "tree shepherd," which itself looks like a tree but is capable of motion, albeit slow motion.

An *adopted word* is one that is taken from another language; *soraismus* is the use of foreign words from various languages and sources, also a type of verse that humorously mingles foreign words with one's "native" language or that makes words in one language conform to the grammatical rules and structures of another language, as in *macaronic verse*. The French (and French Canadians) have set up institutions that, even quite recently, have attempted to keep the French language "pure" by banning adoptions from English. However, when the Norman French invaded and occupied England in the eleventh century, they brought their language with them and imposed many of their words on English, which was radically changed thereby—a very large part of English vocabulary is French-derived. For instance, the Normans brought into English the Old French word "beuf" (from Latin, "bos," "bov"), modern French "bœuf." This word became "beef" in English, and the term "beefsteak" was a *derivation* therefrom, which long ago the French adopted as "bifteck." At the end of the twentieth century the French were worried that the "English" word "beef" was appearing frequently in their language.

Poor choice of words or bad grammatical construction is called *solecism*. *Barbarism* is the use of foreign speech in a literary work or a misuse of one's own native tongue, as in a *malapropism*, named for the malapropos (from the French, *mal apropos*) manner of speaking of Mrs. Malaprop in Richard Brinsley Sheridan's *The Rivals*, who confuses one word inappropriately with another, as in "I would by no means wish a daughter of mine to be a progeny [prodigy] of learning." *Sexisms* are usages that show biases toward one *gender* or the other, traditionally toward the *masculine* at the expense of the *feminine*, for instance, by using "he" or "his" when the *neutral* "one" or "one's" is called for or when the antecedent is a noun of indeterminate gender, such as "teacher" or "doctor."

Vocabulary means all the words of a given language or, in the case of individuals, all the words understood and used by a particular person; for instance, "the vocabulary of Chaucer," which may be ascertained by a study of the words to be found in the works of Geoffrey Chaucer, or "the *King's English*," meaning an educated, proper version of the language. *Lexicography* is the discipline of compiling and defining words for a *lexicon* or *dictionary*; the discipline of *spelling* is *orthography*.

An *epithet* is a characterizing term such as "bright-eyed" in "the bright-eyed baby" or a term used to substitute for the thing described, as in "the virgin queen" rather than "Elizabeth the First" (see *substitutive schemes*). A *transferred epithet* is one that moves a modifier from the word it would ordinarily modify to a *proximal* (nearby) word; for instance, instead of "the **dreary tolling** of the bells" one might use, "the tolling of the **dreary bells**." A *stock epithet* is one that is conventionally used in poems, such as *epics*, *ballads*, *madsongs*, and *nursery rhymes* that are composed extemporaneously, the poets drawing upon such descriptions in the heat of composition, for example, the *Homeric epithet* ("the wine-dark sea") or the Anglo-Saxon *kenning*, which are brief *metaphorical synonyms* composed of two words. In the *Old English* poem "The Wanderer," "chest-locked" means secret; "mind-hoard," secret thoughts; "shield-friends," fellow warriors; "hall-men," clansmen; "youth-yore," yesteryear; "heart's cavern," loneliness; "loaf-lord," a chief who shares his "loaf" (his bounty) with his warriors, and so on.

An *epithetic compound* is two descriptive words made into one (**deathgush**, **thickdark**, **sunbright**). A *portmanteau word* (which is itself a *neologism* coined by Lewis Carroll, author of *Alice in Wonderland*) combines parts of two different words; for instance, "hassle" is perhaps made out of **haggle** and **tussle**. An *oxymoron* is a *descriptive phrase* that combines terms that seem mutually *exclusive* but, in context, are not: "sweet pain," "religious logic," "terrible beauty," "burning chill," and so forth.

Syntax

A *language* is the words of a cultural group arranged in such a way as to form larger units such as *phrases, clauses, sentences, paragraphs, subsections, sections, chapters, volumes, books,* and *series.* The arrangement of words in sentences is called *syntax.* The system of arrangement of words in language is called *grammar. Grammatical parallelism,* or *parallel construction,* is the symmetrical arrangement of words, phrases, and clauses in sentences. For instance, one would not say, "John likes running and to jump." Both these constructions are verbals—that is, nouns derived from verbs—but the first is a gerund and the second an infinitive. Parallel construction demands that both be gerunds or infinitives: "John likes running and jumping," or "John likes to run and jump." A complete sentence is an *independent clause* containing a *subject* and a *predicate.* A subject is a *substantive*—a *noun, pronoun,* or *noun phrase*—that indicates the performer of an action or the recipient of that which is depicted by the *predicate.* A predicate contains an *intransitive verb* (one that does not require an object to complete the action) or a *transitive verb* (one that does require an object) plus all grammatical elements required to complete the action, such as a *predicate nominative* (**I** am **he**), an *object* (Henry lifted the **book**), or *phrases* (the book is **very heavy**). *Incomplete sentences* are *sentence fragments* and are generally words, phrases, and *subordinate clauses* standing alone.

Parallel structure, then, is the structure of symmetrical lists within the sentence and among sentences in a paragraph. These lists may be parts of speech, such as *infinitives* (I like **to run, to**

jump, and **to swim**); *proper nouns* (**Alice**, **Bill**, and **James** like to exercise); *prepositions* (this is a government **of**, **by**, and **for** the people); *phrases* (this is a government **of the people**, **by the people**, and **for the people**); *gerunds* (I like **running**, **jumping**, and **swimming**); *independent clauses* (**I came**, **I saw**, **I conquered**), or any other sentence elements, even *compound elements* such as *subjects* and *predicates* (**Alice**, **Bill**, and **James** like **to run**, **jump**, and **swim**). The controlling word is "symmetrical" lists, for one does not write, "I like to run, jumping, and to swim," even though the sentence makes sense. The elements of the list, of the *catalog* (*frequentatio*), must be in the same form.

A *paragraph* is a manifest subdivision of a text that begins on a fresh, generally indented line, addresses one *concept* or delimited *topic*, and, with the exception of *dialogue*, consists usually of at least two sentences.

The elementary unit of *biblical parallelism* is the *sentence*, called the *verse*. Each sentence is compound, divided into two or sometimes three parts, or *cola* (singular, *colon*), by *caesurae,* or pauses, each colon being syntactically and semantically independent, generally an independent clause. Verses that are divided by a *medial caesura*—that is, by a caesura that divides the sentence in half—may be divided in either a *balanced* or an *unbalanced* manner; that is to say, there may or may not be more words or syllables in one colon than in the other.

Sentence elements of less than independent clausal length also exist, however, and sometimes these are introductory, exclamatory, or rhetorical: "Thus saith the Lord" is a common introductory colon; "O Israel!" is an example of the exclamatory colon to be found in the Bible, and "Selah" or "Amen" are examples of the rhetorical colon.

Three general types of parallelism have been distinguished in the Bible, *semantic parallelism*, *structural parallelism*, and *emblematic parallelism*. In semantic parallelism what is said in the first colon is echoed or repeated either negatively or positively in the second. In structural parallelism there is syntactical (i.e., words) or metrical (i.e., syllables) parallelism in the cola of the verse but not semantic—

that is, there is not parallelism of meaning although there may be the same number of words or of syllables in each half of the parallel. *Emblematic parallelism* is similetic in nature; that is, the first colon is the beginning of a comparison, and the second is the conclusion of the comparison: "As a father pities his children, ‖ so the Lord pities those who fear him" (Ps. 103.13).

There are four major types of parallel grammatical structures that may be isolated in the Bible: *synonymous* and *antithetical parallels* are semantic parallels; *synthetic* and *climactic parallels* are structural parallels. *Synonymous parallelism* breaks each sentence into two cola. The first colon will say something; the second colon will *reiterate,* that is, repeat or paraphrase it. The first sentence of Walt Whitman's poem "I Hear America Singing" is a *synonymous parallel*: "I hear America singing, / **the varied carols I hear**." *Antithetical parallelism* also breaks the verse in half, but the second colon rebuts or contradicts the first: "All things are silent; / **the stillness is a tumult**." Another example is this: "The sun is setting; / **heaven's fire flickers in the west**." *Synthetic parallelism* divides the verse into two cola, but the second gives a consequence of the first: "In the sky there is darkness; / **birds settle out of the air**." *Climactic parallelism* is simply the apex of the symmetrical list; each succeeding colon in the parallel builds to a climax, as in the last sentence of Whitman's poem mentioned above:

> Each singing what belongs to him or her and to none else,
> The day what belongs to the day—at night the party of
>   young fellows, robust, friendly,
> Singing with open mouths their strong melodious songs.

This climax is written in what syntactically is called *paratactic style*, meaning that the elements of its sentences follow one another without distinction as to importance or order, even without overt connection except, minimally, the connective "and." Often, a climactic parallel is simply a *catalog*, a listing of things in parallel. Writing in balanced parallels is called *rounding periods*, and the sentences are *periodic*, meaning that the main clause or the predicate of the clause is withheld until the end of the sentence, as in "Despite his absence and in the presence of his enemies, notwithstanding the fact that he had spurned the occasion, Marlon Brando was given the Oscar." This sentence is also an example of *hypotactic style*, in which the relationships of the parts of the sentence are distinguished by *subordination* and causal links.

The opposite of the periodic sentence is the *loose sentence*, which is **not** a belittling *pejorative term*. A loose sentence is complete grammatically before it reaches its ending, as in the case of a complex sentence beginning with an independent clause and finishing with a dependent clause: "**John left the kitchen and closed the door**, having found what he wanted in the refrigerator."

Perissologia is surplus of language in clauses and phrases, sentences that are too long and oversubordinated, too complex, full of *mannerisms*, as in some of the work of the novelist Henry James, or as in *euphuism*. *Periergia* is oversaying, belaboring a point or description, *overwriting*.

Ciceronian style, after Marcus Tullius Cicero (106–43 B.C.), a great Roman orator, was periodic, cadenced, balanced, and *tropic* (full of *tropes*, figures of speech). The Renaissance *Ciceronians*, who wrote in Latin, refused to use any word not found in the works of Cicero.

Genre

Literature, in the sense that it is used here, is the body of writing, in the language *modes* of *prose*, that is, unmetered language, and *verse*, that is, metered language (see this subject treated at length in *The Book of Forms*) in all *genres*, that is, *types* of writing, that has been deemed to be worthy of study and preservation in the languages of the world but particularly, in the present case, of the English-speaking world. In *metered language* syllables **are** counted or *measured* in *lines* or *stichs*. In *unmetered language* syllables are **not** counted.

The *types of writing* to be found in literature are called *genres*; the primary genres are *fiction, drama, poetry, and nonfiction*—all of these terms are *umbrella terms*, for there are *subgenres* in each category, such as the *novel, novella, novelette* (long story), *short story, short-short story* (very short story), *episode* (one incident or event in a longer work of fiction), and *anecdote* (a short account often of humorous interest) of fiction; the *tragedy, comedy, tragicomedy, melodrama,* and *skit* (a short dramatic presentation of a humorous or satiric turn) of drama; the *autobiography, biography, essay,* and *discourse* of nonfiction, and the *lyric, verse narrative,* and *verse drama* of poetry. **Any** of the *genres* may be written in **either** of the *modes*: there may be prose fiction or verse fiction, prose drama or verse drama, prose poetry or verse poetry, prose nonfiction or verse nonfiction. That group or listing of works of a language, in all the genres and both the modes, which is considered to be central to its literature, is called the *canon.* The word also may mean a list of works of a particular author, genre, literary period, and so forth.

A *writer* of literature is an *author,* and there are as many types of writer as there are genres: novelist, dramatist, essayist, fictionist, poet, critic, scholar, playwright, scriptwriter, speechwriter, journalist, biographer, and so forth.

Much literature is written in the *literary language* of the culture, which is a more refined version of the language than the *vernacular,* which is the ordinary form of the language spoken by most members of an ethnic, cultural, or national group. *Dialect* is the sub-form of a language that is spoken either regionally (e.g., the dialect of American English spoken by the Cajuns of Louisiana) or as a form of a particular language, for instance, the *Romance languages* like Italian, French, Spanish, Romanian, and Portugese, all of which are derived from the *classical language* Latin. Such derived languages are called *vulgar,* to be distinguished from *vulgar language,* which is obscene, base, or otherwise unacceptable language in speech or writing. *Patois* is a close synonym of *dialect,* to be distinguished from *pidgin,* which is a rough amalgam of one or more languages, like the "pidgin English" spoken in parts of the South Pacific islands. *Idiom* has to do with the **peculiar** expressions of a particular language or dialect; that is to say, one cannot understand, from an *etymological analysis* of the expression, either its *derivation* or its logical *definition*. For example, only someone conversant with American English would understand that the expression "She kicked the bucket" means "She died." This is an *Americanism*. "I'll knock you up tonight" is an *Anglicism* meaning "I'll drop by to see you late tonight." As an American expression this latter means something entirely different. Idiom also may refer to the peculiarities of an entire *language*, *dialect*, or *jargon*. *Slang*, which is generally considered to be vulgar language, is an *argot* or *jargon* used by a particular group of people, consisting of a vocabulary that is interspersed with *coined words* and *idiomatic expressions* that identify the speaker with that group, for instance, the African-American *street talk* of the cities of the United States, which is itself derived largely from the argot of jazz musicians. *Argot* is a special vocabulary that is used by a particular group of people, such as physicians; for instance, anyone who watches one of the current hospital shows on television will hear a plethora of argot, much of which will be *gibberish* to the average listener. *Jargon* is a near synonym of argot, as is *lingo*. A *localism* is some form or usage that is peculiar to a *locale*. An *idiolect* is the particular speech pattern of an individual, distinct from his or her culture or group.

Diction

Whereas *syntax* is concerned with the form of the sentence, *diction* has to do with its *tone*—that is, the impression left upon the reader as to the attitude of the author or narrator toward his or her material and the audience and with its *style* (q.v.), or manner of *locution*—"way of speaking." The *level of diction* of the person in the street is usually different from that of a high churchperson. The latter might speak in an "*elevated style*," the former, perhaps, in the *vernacular* or an "*idiomatic style*." These styles are dependent on the levels of diction in which these individuals choose to speak.

In his "Ode: Intimations of Immortality . . ." William Wordsworth wrote, "To me alone there came a thought of grief." A churchperson might say such a thing in such an *affected style* but not likely a laborer because the sentence would not be in *character;* the *level of diction* is *poetic,* not *vernacular* (i.e., everyday, ordinary speech). To be believable as a character, the laborer would have to say something like "A sad thought came to me by my lonesome." The level of diction would thus be in keeping with the character, and the sentence would be an example of *base style* rather than *mean* or *high style.* If an older, well-educated woman character were written into the script, a different version of the same sentence might fit: "A thought of grief came to me alone," an example of *mean style.* Only in the case of the churchperson's sentence is the word order, the syntax, out of normal order. It is "*artificial syntax*"; it does not seem "natural," but it is perfectly good English.

Poetic diction is a manner of speaking designed specifically for writing in the genre of poetry. For instance, in ordinary middle-class speech one might say, "A thought of grief came to me alone." In this sentence the syntax is "normal": the subject of the sentence comes first, then the predicate. But in Wordsworth's ode the syntax is reversed: "To me alone there came a thought of grief." The two sentences say exactly the same thing, but the level of diction of the second is that of nineteenth-century period style because its tone has been "elevated" through syntactical inversion. *Poetic diction* has nothing to do with mode—prose or verse; it can be found in both.

Walt Whitman wrote his poems in prose mode, but his diction was the same elevated poetic diction that William Wordsworth used in verse mode. Opening Whitman's *Complete Poems* at random, one may find examples everywhere: Section 4 of "The Return of the Heroes," for instance, opens with this line: "When late I sang sad was my voice." This passage in normal syntax would be written, "My voice was sad when I sang late[ly]"; or in middle-class diction, "My voice was sad when I sang recently," or even, "When I recently sang my voice was sad." Much more original was the idiosyncratic poetic diction of Emily Dickinson, as in the poem that begins, "Of Course—I prayed— / And did God Care? / He cared as much as on the Air / A Bird had stamped her foot—."

In every era there are always two sorts of poetic diction: that of the *period style,* as we have here been discussing in terms of the nineteenth-century *Romantic style,* and any number of *idiosyncratic styles* invented by individual poets. Such writers we call *stylists.* The nineteenth-century poet Gerard Manley Hopkins sounded little like his contemporaries; here is the opening of "Hurrahing in Harvest":

> Summer ends now; now, barbarous in beauty, the stooks arise
> Around; up above, what wind-walks! what lovely behaviours
> Of silk-sack clouds! has wilder, wilful-wavier
> Meal-drift moulded ever and melted across skies?

Clearly, this is "poetic diction," but in Hopkins's case it has less to do with rearrangements of syntax than with effects on the *sonic level* of poetry (see *The Book of Forms*) and with vocabulary.

The English-language *Neoclassical* or *Augustan period* of the eighteenth century also had both its period style and its idiosyncratic styles. Alexander Pope exemplifies (according to *received opinion*) the best of the period style, as in lines 259–60 of the "Essay on Man,"

> What if the foot, ordain'd the dust to tread,
> Or hand, to toil, aspir'd to be the head?

To flesh this passage out in ordinary prose is to illustrate the difference between *ordinary* and *elevated language*: "What if the foot, ordained to tread the dust; or the hand, ordained to toil, aspired to be the head?" Poetic diction is generally intended to intensify the *aural* (i.e., the listening) experience.

Samuel Johnson's contemporary Christopher Smart sometimes wrote his poems in the poetic diction of the *Neoclassical period style,* as in section 7 of "Hymn to the Supreme Being":

> Yet hold, presumption, nor too fondly climb,
> And thou too hold, O horrible despair!

Considerably before Whitman, Smart also wrote poems in the prose mode; however, in those prose poems his poetic diction turned away from the period style and became idiosyncratic, as in "Of the Sun and the Moon":

> For the Sun's at work to make me a garment & the Moon is at
>   work for my wife.
> For the Wedding Garments of all men are prepared in the Sun
>   against the day of acceptation.
> For the Wedding Garments of all women are prepared in the
>   Moon against the day of their purification.

Here the syntax is normal, but the form of Smart's sentences is based on the scheme *anaphora* (q.v.), and the *sensory level* (i.e., the aspect of language that utilizes figures of speech—see *The Book of Forms*) of the passage is unusual and arresting.

Another poet of that period who wrote in both prose and verse mode, William Blake, had his own poetic diction, but it was the same or quite similar in both modes. The syntax of this so-called *pre-Romantic* poet was more normal than that of the succeeding *Romantics*, as in the beginning of "A Little Girl Lost" from *Songs of Experience*:

> Children of the future age,
> Reading this indignant page,
> Know that in a former time
> Love, sweet love, was thought a crime.

This was a verse poem, of course, but "Creation" is prose:

> I must create a system, or be enslaved by another man's.
> I will not reason compare [an *inversion*: "compare reason"].
>   My business is to create.

The twentieth century also has its period styles and idiosyncratic poetic dictions. W. H. Auden and his group in the pre–World War II period blended formal verse structures with an urbane *conversational style*, as in Auden's "What's the Matter?"

> To lie flat on the back with the knees flexed
> And sunshine on the soft receptive belly
> Or face-down, the insolent spine relaxed,
> No more compelled to cower or to bully,
> Is good; and good to see them passing by
> Below on the white side-walk in the heat,
> The dog, the lady with parcels, and the boy:
> There is the casual life outside the heart.

Writing in this style became what is known as *academic poetry* in the United States, and it persisted even into the so-called *free verse* of the postwar generations: here is the contemporary poet William Stafford in "Adults Only":

> Animals own a fur world;
> people own worlds that are variously, pleasingly, bare.

None of this sounds at all like the poetic diction of Auden's Welsh contemporary, the idiosyncratic Dylan Thomas, who owed more perhaps to Gerard Manley Hopkins than to anyone else, as in "Hold Hard, These Ancient Minutes in the Cuckoo's Month," which is also the first line. The poem continues, "Under the lank, fourth folly on Glamorgan's hill, / As the green blooms ride upward, to the drive of time;" nor does it sound like Theodore Roethke in part 2 of "The Visitant": "Slow, slow as a fish she came, / Slow as a fish coming forward, / Swaying in a long wave;" or the *Postmodern* American poet John Berryman in "Old Man Goes South Again Alone":

> O parakeets & avocets, O immortelles
> & ibis, scarlet under that stunning sun
> deliciously & tired I come
> toward you in orbit, Trinidad! . . .

Literary Movements

It has been postulated that there have always been two kinds of poetry, each of them stemming from prehistory and the *Golden*

Age, which, according to Hesiod (eighth century B.C.) was the original age of humanity, when people lived in harmony with creation and neither fought nor labored, as in the Hebrew Garden of Eden. In the Golden Age "sympathetic magic" (a term of Sir James George Frazer [1854–1941], author of *The Golden Bough*) was the system assumed to prevail in human affairs. The dual laws of *similarity* and *association* were seen to be operative; that is, in the first case, "like begets like" (sprinkle water ritually upon dry earth to produce rain), and in the second case, "things once associated with one another are forever associated" (speak the "secret name" of a god and he or she must do one's bidding). Because there was a god for everything, those whose business it was to placate the deities were required to know the ritual words that would conjure the gods and request or require them to serve humanity's interests. This became *sacred* or *devotional poetry,* which was religiously fervent, prayerful, and supplicatory and was the province of priests and shamans. See Amergin's ancient Irish *chant,* "The Mystery" in *The Book of Forms,* which will give some idea of early *sacred poetry* in Britain.

Words used to entertain—to tell stories, to play games, to remember the traditions and history of an ethnic group, to praise the feats of the leaders, to record the deeds of the warriors, and to honor the dead—were called *social poetry*, and it was the province of the balladeers, the songsters, the grandmothers and grandfathers.

The Age of Gold was followed by the Age of Silver, when men disobeyed the gods and lost their innocence, then by the Age of Bronze, when war was endemic and violence a way of life. At last, there came the Age of Iron, the age of corruption and betrayal, in which mankind lives still.

The Platonic view (after Plato, 427–347 B.C., a student of Socrates [470?–399 B.C.]) sees poetry not as "literature" but as a means to an end. The original end was to placate the gods, but in the modern world it is to catch a glimpse of universal "Truth" or to achieve or express a visionary experience. The American Transcendentalist Ralph Waldo Emerson (1803–1882) said in his essay titled "The Poet" that the poet is "the namer, the sayer," not a person of mere "poetical talents." A poem, then, is not an "*artifice of language*" but a manifestation of "higher" or "cosmic" consciousness. It is not the artful manipulation of words (**not** *social poetry* or *art poetry*) but Truth transcendentally perceived. Thus, poetry is more akin to religious *incantation* than to writing, and the poet is more priest than *maker* (Scottish *makir, bard*). The Platonic poet searches for *vision* through *language*, and "vision" may not be defined as merely "worldview" but as transcendent experience. There are two roads to vision, the *via affirmativa* and the *via negativa*. The former is the "affirmation of images," a poetic avenue that moves outward from the self toward cosmic consciousness; the latter is the "negation of images," an avenue that moves downward into the self toward cosmic awareness. The Book of Genesis says: "In the beginning was the Word, and the Word was with God, and the Word *was* God." The visionary poet wants to know that Word so as to be at One with God (or at least something greater than the self). The path of the intellect is specifically rejected as a means to know the Word; *intuition* and *inspiration* (nervous excitement) are the appropriate means. In other words, Platonic poetry is *sacred poetry,* or *carmen*—inspired, prophetic, or oracular song. Such poets were classically called *vates, vatic poets.* However, all serious poetry of whatever tradition may be considered to be essentially religious in that the poet is interested in the human condition, and it is through poetry that the poet's perception of this condition is reflected and mankind's relationship to the world and to the universe is sought.

Poetry having as its base the view that poetry is *language artifice* is based on the precepts of Aristotle (384–322 B.C.), a student of Plato who studied the literary works of his day, particularly *tragedy*, and abstracted certain qualities and elements that many of them had in common, including the *unities*, the *mimetic* nature of art, and the principles of *proportion* and *balance*. These topics are covered more fully in the discussion of *tragedy* in the chapter titled "The Genres of Drama."

The *Neoclassical* period of the eighteenth century set up these qualities as ideals so that succeeding periods of literature have seen

Aristotelian poetry as being primarily of the intellect and not of the emotions, but such poetry is not truly Aristotelian or classical; it is, in effect, *ideational verse*. Aristotle did not reject vision in the Platonic sense but would include as part of the definition of vision a "worldview." Aristotelian poetry is *classical* or *Apollonian* poetry, after Apollo, the god of music, medicine, poetry, and prophecy; in other words, it is *social poetry*. The Apollonian impulse is to create order and beauty from existence.

It should be noted that the definition of Aristotelian poetry is broad enough to include Platonic poetry, but the reverse is not true. *Platonic poetry* is *Dionysian poetry,* after Dionysus, the Greek god of revelry, wine, and fertility. When a Platonic poet is moved to write, he or she is filled with *divine afflatus*, passionate frenzy, the *furor poeticus*—poetic drunkenness. The Dionysian impulse is to express a sense of the chaos and irrationality of human existence. Both Apollonian and Dionysian poets are in the care of the *Muses*, the nine daughters of *Mnemosyne*, goddess of *memory*, and Zeus. The Muses of poetry, who live on the slopes of the sacred mount *Parnassus*, are *Calliope*, the muse of *epic poetry*; *Euterpe*, of *lyric poetry*; *Erato*, of *erotic poetry; Melpomene*, of *tragedy; Polyhymnia*, of *sacred poetry; Terpsichore*, of *song and dance;* and *Thalia*, of *comedy*. The other muses are *Clio*, muse of *history*, and *Urania*, muse of *astronomy*. The poet rides the winged horse named *Pegasus,* who, with its hoof, struck open Hippocrene, the Muses' well of *inspiration* on Mount Helicon.

The *Alexandrian period* was *circa* 330–30 B.C., and the term *Alexandrian* pertains to *Hellenist*—that is, influenced by Greek culture—writers of that period living in Alexandria, Egypt, which was a center for learning and a repository of many of the world's greatest manuscripts. The *neo-Platonists* were a school of philosophers of *circa* 200–400 who posited that all good emanated from the Absolute, which was the origin of all things.

England and the British Isles have been home to several *literary languages* over the centuries. The earliest inhabitants of the British Isles were the Picts, who were driven by the Romans into the outlands of the North, where they merged with the Celts. The *Pictish* language was extinct by the tenth century and is known primarily by a few place-names. Prior to the sixth century B.C. the Isles were invaded by Celtic tribes from the European Continent, and their well-developed languages were eventually known as *Erse* (*Gaelic*), *Welsh, Manx,* and *Cornish,* which has been extinct since the eighteenth century.

The Romans began to invade by 55 B.C. bringing the classical language and literature of the *Latin* tongue with them, reaching the peak of their rule by the first half of the third century A.D. By the fifth century, Rome had withdrawn its support of its legions in Britain, and the Isles were subjected to a series of invasions from the Continent by Germanic tribes and to internal pressures from the North by the Celtic tribes. England became a checkerboard of fiefdoms and petty kingdoms with numerous related Germanic languages spoken by tribes such as the Angles, the Saxons, the Danes and the Jutes.

The so-called *Dark* or *Middle Ages* ensued, which, by one reckoning, extended from *circa* 476 A.D. to about the year 1000 and, by another, the period from the end of classical civilization to the rebirth of learning in the West, the *Renaissance.* The phrase *Anglo-Saxon England* describes the period from 450 A.D. to 1066, when the Scandinavian tribes were making their incursions into the British Isles and establishing enclaves and colonies, and this period was marked by the installation of the language now called *Old English.* By the eighth century, in all probability, the first major poem in a European *vernacular language* (as distinguished from classical Latin and Greek) had been written. The poem takes its title from its *heroic protagonist,* the legendary *Beowulf.*

Norman England began in the year 1066, when William the Conqueror of Normandy (1027?–87), after having been promised the English throne by Edward the Confessor, his cousin, invaded England and defeated Harold II at the Battle of Hastings. From this point, French was the official court, literary, and legal language of England, although Latin remained the language of the church. Such poets as Marie de France of England (1160?–1215?) wrote in the French language and in syllabic prosody while, in the countryside, the native poets continued to write in strong-stress prosody. (For explanations and examples of these terms, see *The Book of Forms*.) "Norman" means "Northman," and these people were of the same racial stock as the Englishmen they had conquered, the difference being that, in England, Norse culture had prevailed over the Roman and Celtic, whereas on the Continent the invading Norse had instead adopted French culture. Thus, by the eleventh century the literary languages of Britain had been Celtic, Latin, Germanic, and French. Each of these languages had a *literary tradition*.

Courtly love was a medieval and Renaissance movement and convention that was chivalric in nature and had as its basis the idealization of illicit love and womankind, generally the married kind. The would-be lover, a knight or courtier, addressed his noble paramour with unrequited or virtuous passion, generally in poetry, and his complaints were judged and arbitrated by an aristocratic Court of Love.

The Latin prosody of the Romans was, early on, an adaptation of the Greek *quantitative accentual-syllabic prosody* and, later, the biblical prose system we call grammatical parallelism. The Celts wrote their poetry in a *prosody* (a **system** of *composition*) that we call *syllabics*; the Germanic prosody was a system we call *alliterative accentuals* (*Anglo-Saxon prosody*) or *strong-stress prosody*, and the French system for writing poetry was a different form of *syllabics* from that of the Celts. By the fourteenth century all of these prosodies had been in use in Britain for centuries, giving the English language an exceptionally broad prosodic base, and *rhyme* (originally spelled *rime* but corrupted by confusion with the word *rhythm*) had been added by the Normans to the stock of sounds the Anglo-Saxons used in their language music.

Over the course of three centuries an enormous French vocabulary blended slowly but surely with the Anglo-Saxon tongue, and by the time of Geoffrey Chaucer this amalgam had resulted in a new dialect (actually, a new series of English dialects) that we now call *Middle English*. The *Anglo-Norman period* lasted between about 1100 and 1400. By the fifteenth century not only had Norman French and Old English merged, but the *Age of Chaucer* was marked by a great flowering of poetry in England, some of it written in alliterative accentuals, as in the work of William Langland (1332?–1400), author of *The Vision of William Concerning Piers the Plowman,* and "The Gawain Poet," about whom nothing is known except that he or she is very likely the author of both the elegiac *The Pearl* and the great *alliterative romance* or *epic, Gawain and the Green Knight.* Some of the literature of this period was written in French and Latin, as in two of the works of John Gower (1325?–1408), and some of it in English, in the new prosody, the invention of Gower in his English poem, *Confessio Amantis,* and of Geoffrey Chaucer (1340?–1400) in all of his work, including his masterpiece, *The Canterbury Tales.*

For one hundred years, between the death of Geoffrey Chaucer and the beginning of the English Renaissance in 1500, accentual-syllabic verse was largely forgotten in England, but it was kept alive by Thomas Hoccleve (1369?–1450?) and the so-called Scottish Chaucerians (the Scots language even today is a version of Middle English), who included Robert Henryson (ca. 1480) and William Dunbar (1460?–1520?).

In England itself during this century the prosodic system had slipped halfway back to accentual prosody in the *"folk poetry"* of the *"border balladeers"* (on the border between England and Scotland), who wrote in the system we now call *podic prosody,* a misnomer, for "pod" means "foot" and there are no *verse feet* involved. (For an example of this sort of poem see "Tom O'Bedlam's Song" in *The Book of Forms.*)

While he was in Bruges learning the ways of the new invention called the printing press, Thomas Caxton (1422?–91) printed the first book in English, his 1475 translation from the French of Raoul le Febre's *The Recuyell of the Historyes of Troye.* The next year he moved back to England and set up his press in Westminster and over fourteen years published many translations and other works, including *The Temple of Glass* by John Lydgate (1370?–1451?), several of Chaucer's works, including *The Canterbury Tales* (1478 and 1484), Gower's *Confessio Amantis,* and in 1485, *Le Morte d'Arthur* by Thomas Malory (ca. 1470).

The *Renaissance* had begun in Italy in the fourteenth century, and it spread to the rest of Europe over the next two hundred years, reaching Britain in the sixteenth century. The Renaissance was marked not only by a rediscovery of Aristotle's scientific method, Galen's medicine, and other classical learning from ancient Greece and Rome but also by a revival of Arabic and Hebrew learning. By the beginning of the sixteenth century, Middle English had become what we call *Modern English*, and Chaucer's accentual-syllabics was rediscovered and used in some of the poetry of the transitional poet John Skelton (1460–1529), who also wrote in podic prosody, and in the work and theory of early English Renaissance poets like Thomas Wyatt (1503–42) and Henry Howard (1517–47). The *courtly makers* were English Renaissance court poets of the time of Henry VIII (r. 1509–47) whose children were his successors, ending with Elizabeth I (r. 1558–1603), Muse of the *Elizabethan Age*.

John Skelton has been called the last of the English medieval poets by some, and by others the first of the English Renaissance poets. No doubt he was both, for he wrote not only in podic prosody, like the anonymous English poets since Chaucer, but in accentual-syllabic prosody as well, like the Scottish Chaucerians, Chaucer himself, and almost all other English poets up through the nineteenth century.

This era was followed by the *Jacobean period*, the era of James VI of Scotland, who succeeded Elizabeth as James I of England (r. 1603–25). The *School of Spenser*, which was influenced by the archaism and medievalism of Edmund Spenser (1552–99), included William Alexander (1577?–1640), William Browne (1590?–1645?), John Davies (1569–1626), William Drummond of Hawthornden (1585–1649), Giles Fletcher (1588?–1623), Phineas Fletcher (1582–1650), and George Wither (1588–1667). The *University Wits* was a group of young writers, primarily playwrights, who, toward the end of the sixteenth century, gathered in London to write and experiment with plays. Included were Robert Greene (1558?–92), Thomas Kyd (1558–94), Christopher Marlowe (1564–93), Thomas Nashe (1567–1601), and George

Peele (1556?–96). The *Tribe of Ben* was a *coterie* of seventeenth century *epigones*—imitators—who followed the classical precepts of Ben Jonson (1572–1637), the great contemporary of William Shakespeare (1564–1616).

The chief members of the "Tribe" were also known as the *Cavalier Poets*, including Robert Herrick (1591–1674), Thomas Carew (1595?–1639), Richard Lovelace (1618–57?), and John Suckling (1609–42). The school of *Metaphysical Poets* in late-sixteenth and early-seventeenth-century England was a suborder of the *Caroline Poets* of the reign of Charles I; they included John Donne (1572–1631), George Herbert (1593–1633), Andrew Marvell (1621–78), and Henry Vaughan (1622–95). All these writers were formalists, but the Metaphysical Poets used the *conceit* (an archaic form of the word "concept"), a *controlling image* or *extended metaphor*, in their work, which also relied on such rhetorical tropes as *irony* and *paradox*.

Another style of the period was *euphuism*, after the protagonist in the novel *Euphues* by John Lyly (1554?–1606), characterized by excessive ornamentation (*aureate language*), highly wrought *parallelism*, many sonic techniques such as *alliteration*, and extreme elegance of *syntax* and *diction*. The *inkhornists* were those who advocated introducing Greek and Latin terms directly into the English vocabulary. They were successful in this endeavor in the case of many rhetorical and poetic terms, including the Greek names of verse feet, even though these were basically inappropriate to English language prosody. A similar Spanish style of the era was *Gongorism*, named after its inventor, Luis de Góngora y Argote (1561–1627); in Italy, *Marinism*, after Giambattista Marino (1569–1625) was the term used. The Greek model for such styles was that of Isocrates (436–338 B.C.). All these styles are examples of "*fine writing*" or *preciosity*, often marked by *sigmatism*, the overuse of sibilants.

Hudibrastic, after *Hudibras*, a *mock epic* by Samuel Butler (1612–80), is a term that refers to a type of savage satire written in rough tetrameter couplets (see *The Book of Forms*). Butler's poem was aimed at Oliver Cromwell (1599–1658) and the Puritans, who overthrew the British monarchy in the English civil war (1642–

48) and ruled during the Commonwealth period or *Interregnum* (1649–59) until the beginning of the *Restoration* in 1660.

The *Battle of the Books* was a late-seventeenth-century debate over the relative merits of the ancient classical writers and those of the contemporary period. It was during the Renaissance that two things occurred: the wisdom of the ancients was recovered, and the age of science dawned; the debate was about which was most important, *lore* or *progress*. The first English principals of this debate were William Temple, who, in his *An Essay upon the Ancient and Modern Learning* (1690) took the side of the classical writers, and William Wotton, who, in *Reflections upon Ancient and Modern Learning* (1694), took the opposite view.

Neoclassicism, the manifestation of the twentieth century poet T. S. Eliot's theory of the *dissociation of sensibility*, was a resurgence, in late-seventeenth- and early-eighteenth-century *Augustan* literature, of the *Aristotelian ideals* of *logical thinking, formalism, control,* and *balance.* Such a program was espoused by Jonson and later by Dryden. It became dominant during the eighteenth century in the work of Alexander Pope (1688–1744), reached its zenith with the *Age of Sensibility* or, alternatively, the *Age of* (Samuel) *Johnson,* and began to wane in the nonfiction of Mary Wollstonecraft (1759–97) and the "*pre-Romantic*" poetry of Robert Burns (1759–96) and William Blake (1757–1827).

The *Scriblerus Club*, founded in 1714 by Jonathan Swift, with members that included John Arbuthnot (1667–1735), Henry Saint John, Lord Bolingbroke (1678–1751), William Congreve (1670–1729), John Gay (1685–1732), and Alexander Pope (1688–1744), had as its goal the lampooning of bad writing and bad writers. Its primary document was *The Memoirs of the Extraordinary Life, Works, and Discoveries of Martinus Scriblerus*, the main author of which was Arbuthnot.

Samuel Johnson (1709–84) began his London literary career as a *Grub Street hack*—one who writes for money only, producing *potboilers*—and turned himself autodidactically into the complete *person of letters*. He published his definitive *A Dictionary of the English Language* in 1755 and his multivolume *Lives of the Poets* from

1779 to 1781. He was immortalized further by the biography written by James Boswell (1740–95). The *Literary Club*, organized by Sir Joshua Reynolds in 1764, was composed of members of Johnson's circle of friends. There were seven charter members, including Reynolds, Johnson, Edmund Burke (1729–97) and Oliver Goldsmith (1730?–74).

A synonym for the Neoclassical or Augustan period (*the Age of Reason*) is *the Enlightenment*, but this term is more properly applied to a religious view of the era, which held that humanity can attain perfectibility on earth without waiting to achieve it in heaven. This doctrine was a part of the religious *Deism* of the age, a belief that God had created Earth and its creatures but was no longer directly involved with his Creation; it was now up to humankind to act rationally and decently and to preserve the world and society so that they remain useful and viable.

Primitivism is a belief that humanity was a much better creature in the earliest stages of its existence, and the closer it remains to its origins, the purer it is. The *cult of the Noble Savage* of the eighteenth century idolized the American Indian and other "primitive" cultures, and poetry written by rustic or working-class poets such as Robert Burns and John Clare (1793–1864) was lionized.

In North America there was beginning to be a literary culture. The *Connecticut Wits*, sometimes inappropriately called the *Hartford Wits*, was a group made up of Joel Barlow (1754–1812), Timothy Dwight (1752–1817), and John Trumbull (1750–1831), the three most prominent members, and of others, including Richard Alsop; Theodore Dwight, Timothy's brother; Lemuel Hopkins; David Humphreys; and Elihu Hubbard Smith.

The *literature of sensibility* was a late-eighteenth-century sentimental response to Thomas Hobbes's assertion that human beings are driven not by any form of altruism but only by self-interest and the impulse to achieve social status and personal power. Critics posited in opposition to this theory the affirmation that people are innately good and sympathetic and that they are sensible to the situations of others. The *Gothic Revival* of the same period refers to literature that took a morbid if elegant interest in the decaying, the macabre, and the grotesque, as in Horace Walpole's (1717–97) Gothic novel, *The Castle of Otranto,* and a century later, Mary Shelley's (1797–1851) *Frankenstein.* This genre continues to be produced, a twentieth-century offshoot being called *Southern Gothic,* as in the work of Carson McCullers (1917–67) or of William Faulkner (1897–1962) in a story such as "A Rose for Emily" (q.v.). One of the manifestations of the Gothic Revival was the *Graveyard School* of poetry, which included *elegists* such as Thomas Gray (1716–71), whose "Elegy in a Country Church-yard" was the most widely read poem in the English language for many years, well into the twentieth century. The *Preromantic poets* of the Augustan age, such as William Blake (1757–1827) and Robert Burns (1759–96), exhibited certain tendencies that would become dominant in the succeeding *Romantic Period.*

Romanticism is a term later used to label the work of early-nineteenth-century English writers such as William Wordsworth (1770–1850), Samuel Taylor Coleridge (1772–1834), George Gordon (1788–1824), Percy Bysshe Shelley (1792–1822), and John Keats (1795–1821). It had as its dual purpose to make the mundane seem vivid and to make the eerie seem real. The central document of Romanticism, which was a term never used by the writers of the Romantic movement (no more than the term "Preromantic"), was the preface by Wordsworth to the 1800 (second) edition of *Lyrical Ballads*, a book of poems co-authored by Wordsworth and Coleridge. Wordsworth proposed to write poems in the language of ordinary people, rather than in the *artificial diction* of the preceding century. Nevertheless, the common person could not be expected to write poetry, only the "great man" (*sic*) or "great poet" could do so, which was one of the Romantic concepts that the contemporary novelist Thomas Love Peacock satirized. However, this person had earlier been described by George Puttenham (ca. 1529–90) during the Renaissance, in his *The Arte of English Poesie* (see bibliography), where the *euphantasiote* was described as one who is "illuminated with the brightest irradiations of knowledge and of the verity and due proportion of things." The *Cockney School* was a pejorative name used by Tory critics for those poets and writers, including Keats, Shelley, Leigh Hunt (1784–1859), and William Hazlitt (1778–1830), who were prone to rhyme words with a Cockney accent, to use base diction, and to be deficient in sensibility and manners.

The satirical novelist Thomas Love Peacock (1785–1866), in his essay "The Four Ages of Poetry," rearranged Hesiod's ages of man somewhat and applied them mockingly to the poetry of his time, particularly that of William Wordsworth; however, Peacock's satire was also directed at the work of the other *Lake Poets*, a school that took its name from the region around the northern Cumberland lakes of England where this group, which included Samuel Taylor Coleridge and Robert Southey (1774–1843), spent varying amounts of time.

The *Knickerbocker School* of writers existed during the first part of the nineteenth century in New York City. Members included William Cullen Bryant (1794–1878), James Fenimore Cooper (1789–1851), Joseph Rodman Drake (1795–1820), Fitzgreene Halleck (1790–1867), and Washington Irving (1783–1859). The *Schoolroom Poets* were those American poets of the nineteenth century whose work, during the early twentieth century, was almost exclusively the only American poetry taught in grammar schools and high schools. They included William Cullen Bryant, John Greenleaf Whittier (1807–92), John Godfrey Saxe (1816–1887), Oliver Wendell Holmes (1809–94), Henry Wadsworth Longfellow (1807–82), James Russell Lowell (1819–91), and Ralph Waldo Emerson (1803–82). Poets such as Walt Whitman, who were considered either too vulgar or too lightweight by the *schoolmarms* of the period, were not taught in the classroom, which generally followed a curriculum that was not at odds with the *genteel tradition* of literature, that is, literature as moral uplift. This is a form of *censorship,* or banning of certain texts by members of the community, who do not wish children to be exposed to "moral corruption" or literary "indecency." Nothing was to be taught that was not acceptable to the "*feminine sensibility.*" The ally of the genteel tradition is the *Philistine*, who cares nothing for art or the life of the mind but only for materialism and practicality.

Grundyism is a term that applies in this situation, for Mrs. Grundy, who does not actually appear as a character in the drama *Speed the Plough* by the American colonist Thomas Morton (ca. 1600–ca. 1647), is nevertheless a pervasive influence on the other characters who constantly ask, "What would Mrs. Grundy say?"

The *Transcendental Club*, founded in Boston in 1836 at the home of George Ripley (1802–80), met thereafter at odd times and informally at the home of Ralph Waldo Emerson. Members included Amos Bronson Alcott (1799–1888), William Ellery Channing (1780–1842), Margaret Fuller (1810–50), Nathaniel Hawthorne (1804–64), and Henry David Thoreau (1817–62) among others.

The *Victorian period* overlapped and followed the Romantic period, corresponding roughly with the reign of Queen Victoria. Swinburne and the Brownings were "Victorian" in terms of chronology, but "Victorian" has pejorative overtones of prudishness, fussy gentility, and conformity, which certainly did not fit Swinburne; therefore, suborders of literature are generally conjured to distinguish the many viewpoints and schools that flourished throughout the period.

The critic Walter Pater (1839–94) introduced into England from France some of the precepts of *Aestheticism* (q.v.). Pater was interested in style and artifice and in sensual experience. Others of those who shared such interests were the *Pre-Raphaelite Brotherhood*, a school of London-area poets and artists of the mid-nineteenth century organized by Dante Gabriel Rossetti (1828–82).

Later in the century in both France and England the *Age of Decadence* ensued. Its participants showed signs of exaggerated aestheticism, ornamentation, and a search for ever-heightened sensation. In England, Oscar Wilde (1854–1900) and Algernon Charles Swinburne (1837–1909) were counted decadents. Wilde's novel *The Picture of Dorian Gray* depicted the effects of decadence on a man who remained forever young while his portrait grew older and showed in its face the ravages of his degradation.

Realism, like Romanticism, was a literary program of the nineteenth century that set out to write about ordinary people in ordi-

nary situations, using ordinary language. The French novelist
Gustave Flaubert, the Russian Fyodor Dostoevsky, the English-
woman George Eliot, and the American Stephen Crane were all
Realists. *Regionalists* are those realists who used details from a specific *locale* or area to give their work *local color*. Writers who used
slice of life technique presented the reader with unedited and unex-
purgated, almost "photographic" reality. *Critical realism* is a term
distinguishing between realistic fiction and such fiction intended
to criticize the society it discusses. The *slave narrative* of early- to
mid-nineteenth-century America was an account of a former
slave, sometimes almost wholly fictive but masquerading as autobiography, written in the service of abolition. The *Kailyard* school
of Scotland, which included J. M. Barrie (1860–1937), used dialect during the late nineteenth century in depictions of common
people in everyday situations.

In the twentieth century, Realism was supplanted by a bleaker
program, *Naturalism*, which maintained that people's lives were
controlled by external forces, such as economics or environment,
or by people's inner limitations. Naturalism might perhaps be defined as "*Marxism* [after the *Communist* theories of Karl Marx]
without hope." Another synonym for Naturalism is *Determinism*;
the American novelists Frank Norris and James T. Farrell were
Naturalists.

Impressionism was a style both in art and in literature of the
1870s in France and elsewhere. The term indicates that the sensory level was to be used in such a way as to evoke mood and to
suggest rather than to state. The American Modernist poet Alfred
Kreymborg (1883–1966), in his poem "Nun Snow," was an Im-
pressionist, as were Amy Lowell and Hilda Doolittle in much of
their work, although they are both thought of as *Imagists*.

The French *Symbolists* of the late nineteenth century included
Charles Baudelaire (1821–67), Stéphane Mallarmé (1842–98),
and Paul Verlaine (1844–96), who were interested in the *archetype*
(or *prototype*, the original model of something), and Arthur Rim-
baud (1854–91), whose work subsequently influenced the *Surrealists*. The Symbolists were themselves influenced by the American

poet Edgar Allan Poe (1809–49) as regards both technique and the usages of the *sensory level* of their poetry (see *The Book of Forms*).

Jungian psychology, named after its founder, Karl Jung, diverged from *Freudianism*, founded by Sigmund Freud, in that it disagreed with Freud's dictum that all neuroses and psychoses could be traced to a sexual root. Jung maintained that there were other human drives besides the sexual, including hunger, power, anger, and so forth. Each of these drives has its *symbol* or *archetype*, and these remanifest themselves in each generation because they reside in the *race memory* or *collective unconscious*. Thus, the Greek authority symbol Zeus remanifested itself as the Roman Jupiter, the Hebrew Jahweh, and the Christian Jehovah. Or to turn to the distaff, the Greek goddess of love, Aphrodite, became, successively, the Roman Venus, the Italian Mona Lisa, and, more recently, Marilyn Monroe and Madonna. The symbols of the Symbolists were of this magnitude.

The *Celtic Renaissance* took place in Ireland during the late nineteenth century with the participation of such writers as the poets William Butler Yeats (1865–1939), and Æ (George William Russell, 1867–1935), and the playwrights John Millington Synge (1871–1909) and Lady Isabella Augusta Persse Gregory (1852–1932), one of the founders and the director of the Abbey Theatre in Dublin.

The Edwardian period extended from 1901 to 1910, the reign of Edward VII. It was characterized in literature by its anti-Victorian tenor and iconoclasm. The playwright George Bernard Shaw (1856–1950), the novelist Joseph Conrad (1857–1924), and the poet-novelist Thomas Hardy (1840–1928) are often counted Edwardian writers.

The period in England between 1910 and 1936, when George V was monarch, is called the *Georgian era*, and certain poets of the second rank who looked back toward Victorianism rather than ahead or even to more viable movements of their own period are called *Georgian poets*. Their more *avant-garde*—that is, experimental—contemporaries have come to be called *Modernists*, like the *Bloomsbury Group* of London: Virginia Woolf (1882–1941), Lytton

Strachey (1880–1932), E. M. Forster (1879–1970), and others. *Modernism* was a movement of the first half of the twentieth century that was characterized by formal and stylistic experimentation, rebellion against Victorian standards of literature, morality, and style, and the sense that the present, unlike the past, which had seemed to have a religious center, was adrift and searching for a direction. Americans like Gertrude Stein (1874–1946), who left the United States to escape the middle-class Victorian mores of the period, called themselves "The Lost Generation." They included such people as Ernest Hemingway (1899–1961) and F. Scott Fitz-Gerald (1896–1940).

Imagism, the original Modernist movement, founded by the poet Ezra Pound, discovered its best *slogan*, perhaps, in the remark by one of its members, William Carlos Williams, that there ought to be "no ideas but in things." This school believed that the *sensory level* of poetry was the most important, and it underplayed the *sonic level*. T. S. Eliot's notion of the *objective correlative* was that, if one chose the proper *object* or *vehicle* for one's metaphor, one would not need to mention the *subject* or *tenor* at all, for one would have chosen the object that is relative to the idea being expressed; the idea would be clearly seen in the image itself.

Much of the poetry of *Modernism* returned to the Latin practice of writing *prose poems* in grammatic parallel prosody, which had been kept alive in English literature by such poets as the Renaissance translators of the *King James Bible* (*The Song of Songs*, *The Psalms*), the eighteenth-century poets Christopher Smart (*Jubilate Agno*) and William Blake (*The Marriage of Heaven and Hell*), both of whom wrote poetry in prose and verse alike; the nineteenth century English *poetaster* Martin Farquhar Tupper (*Proverbial Philosophy*); American poets Edgar Allan Poe (*Eureka!*) and Walt Whitman (*Leaves of Grass*), and the twentieth-century *Imagistes* led by Ezra Pound (*The Cantos*), who popularized *dispersing* the grammatic parallels by *line-phrasing* (or *lineating* them): by breaking the independent clauses into phrases, each of which was assigned a "line" to give it the appearance of verse, called *free verse* after the nineteenth-century French term *vers libre*.

T. S. Eliot (1888–1965) believed that the metaphysical poets were the last to have a "unified *sensibility*"—that is to say, a balance of mind and emotion—which manifested itself in their work. According to Eliot, in the subsequent late seventeenth century and all of the eighteenth, a *dissociation of sensibility* occurred, particularly among the *Restoration Poets*, the chief of whom was John Dryden (1631–1700), and people wrote only with their minds, not with their feelings, until the Romantic period of the early nineteenth century, when a reaction set in and poets wrote with their emotions, not with their minds.

This is much too pat a theory, however, for in all of history since the Classical Greek period there have been both "romantic" and "classical" poets. Nevertheless, it is true that in some ages one predominates over the other, and in the United States the two points of view have tended to war with one another ever since the Platonic theories of the nineteenth century *transcendentalist* critic Ralph Waldo Emerson (1803–82) gave rise to the *antiformalist*, extreme Platonism of the prose poet Walt Whitman (1819–92) whose influence on the Modernists was vast.

Symbolists of the early twentieth century were the Irish poet William Butler Yeats, who was converted from the Celtic Twilight to Modernism by Ezra Pound and others; the Anglo-American T. S. Eliot and the American Wallace Stevens (1879–1955), whose *metapoetry* (poetry about poetry) subsequently influenced later schools.

As an example of the Symbolist method, consider the poem titled "Not Ideas about the Thing but the Thing Itself" by Wallace Stevens. The first stanza is a statement:

> At the earliest ending of winter,
> In March, a scrawny cry from outside
> Seemed like a sound in his mind.

The poem is a *narrative*, then, and if it were a piece of prose fiction one would say that its *narrator* is the author telling a story in the *third person* from a *single angle* (one person is followed in the poem) and with *subjective access*—that is to say, the author knows what is going on not only in the protagonist's vicinity but in his mind as well.

The second stanza tells the reader that the protagonist of the poem was sure, despite the sound's seeming location "in his mind," that its true origin was at dawn or just before, "In the early March wind."

> The sun was rising at six,
> No longer a battered panache above snow . . .
> It would have been outside.

Of course it would. The season was advancing, and the sun no longer appeared to be a bedraggled plume of feathers worn by the winterscape. But there is a suggestion—an *overtone*—here that the bird, the utterer of the cry, might itself be a panache, battered or otherwise; it might, in fact, be the voice of the rising sun.

The protagonist could be sure that the sound he had heard was not the echo of a dream, a voice "not from the vast ventriloquism / Of sleep's faded papier-mâché" because surely "The sun was coming from outside."

"That scrawny ['battered,' 'bedraggled'] cry" was the utterance of "A chorister" whose note, a "c[,] preceded the choir[,]"—that is to say, the full chorus of daylight. And it was, indeed, "part of the colossal sun" after all, the voice of the world of reality, not of dream or imagination, which would reach full throat in the daylight when the sun would be "surrounded by its choral rings, / Still far away." The *pun* on "choral rings" is evident. The sun is a volcanic atoll in the oceanic sky, surrounded by sound and living things. "It was like / A new knowledge of reality," Stevens says in a figure of speech, a *simile*. The thing itself, the "scrawny cry," was like a knowledge of reality to the listener at dawn, but it was reality in and of itself. That is the thing the *listener*, the *narrator*, and the *reader* must understand.

Many of the Modernists were Jungians, but they were also influenced by Freudianism, including the British novelist and poet

D. H. Lawrence (1885–1930) and the Irish writer James Joyce (1882–1941). One experimental technique of the period was *stream of consciousness,* which attempted to convey to the reader the impression of how a mind actually works, as Joyce did in his prose epic *Ulysses*, Woolf did in *The Waves*, and William Faulkner did in his novel *The Sound and the Fury*:

its late you go on home
what
you go on home its late
all right
her clothes rustled I didn't move they stopped rustling
are you going in like I told you
I didn't hear anything
Caddy
yes I will if you want me to I will
I sat up she was sitting on the ground her hands clasped about her knee
go on to the house like I told you
yes I'll do anything you want me to anything

Existentialism, a modern *nihilism* that maintained that each individual was alone in a meaningless world and responsible for his or her own actions and well-being, was the order of the day. The existentialist approaches the problem of human existence as a personal confrontation with a reality that is chaotic, meaningful only through an effort of personal will—in Wallace Stevens's terms, "a rage for order." Stevens also believed, and stated in the first line of his poem "The Snowman," that "One must have a *mind of winter*" (italics added), the state of objectivity of observation that an *artificer* must cultivate to produce art and order out of the chaos of existence, the striking of balance between intellect and emotion (see *sensibility*) in the artist and in the artifice. A central existential document of Modernism is T. S. Eliot's *The Waste Land*.

Another movement of the Age of Modernism was *Expressionism*, which intended to distort reality so as to express the inner senses or experiences of the characters in drama, as in Eugene O'Neill's play *The Hairy Ape* or the film *The Cabinet of Dr. Caligari*.

Dadaism (1916–23), a French movement founded by Jean (or Hans) Arp (1887–1966) and others, ridiculed conventional values by producing works marked by nonsense, caricature, and nonconformity. *Dada prosody* produced poetry based on the principle of randomness. A Dada author might take something he, she, or someone else had written, cut out each word separately, and drop them all into a sack. The sack would then be shaken and each word extracted from it and pasted on a sheet of paper in random-length lines. Although the results were often unreadable, at other times they were oddly interesting, and even the Dada method is a *prosody*; its organizing principles are not absolutely random, for one needs certain things: (1) words, (2) a bag, (3) paper and paste, and (4) someone to drop the words into the bag, shake it up, extract the words one by one, and arrange them in lines (a *maker*). The Gallic nation seems always to have had a penchant for chaotic art, for the *descort* is an old French form of *logaoedic* or *ibycean* verse whose only requirement is that each line of the poem be different from every other in all ways; that is to say, discordant. The descort mixes meters, line lengths, and stanza lengths and is itself of no fixed length.

Surrealism, which succeeded Dadaism, was a movement in the arts and in literature that distorted reality in ways that called attention to the absurdity of existence. One of the great Surrealists among writers was Franz Kafka, whose protagonist in "Metamorphosis" woke up one morning to discover he had been turned into an insect. Kafka wrote about his distortions in an ordinary style, which made his situations seem all the more bizarre. Federico García Lorca in his plays approached the surreal in much the same way, for his Spanish personae did not speak in a distorted manner. The Colombian novelist Gabriel García Márquez was a late, *Postmodern* Surrealist.

The Fugitives was a school of American poets and writers associated with a *literary magazine, The Fugitive,* published at Vanderbilt University in Nashville, Tennessee, from 1922 to 1925. Members of the group were Donald Davidson (1893–1968), Merrill Moore (1903–57), John Crowe Ransom (1888–1974), Laura Riding

(1901–41), Allen Tate (1899–1979), and Robert Penn Warren (1905–88), some of whom were also associated with the politically oriented southern *Agrarians* and with *the New Criticism*.

The *Angry Young Men* of the 1950s in the United Kingdom was a group of novelists and playwrights, some of them of working-class origin, who expressed hostility toward the Establishment in their work. Members of the group were the novelists Kingsley Amis (b. 1922), John Braine (1922–86), and Alan Sillitoe (b. 1928), and the playwright John Osborne (b. 1929).

In the United States the Black Mountain school originated at the sometime Black Mountain College of Asheville, North Carolina, in the 1950s and gave rise to an *antiacademic* academy, whose "Rector," Charles Olson (1910–70), was the center of attraction for many of the disaffiliated writers of the period, including many who were known in other contexts as the *Beats* or the *Beat Generation* and the *San Francisco School*. All of these "*beatnik*" writers stood against the poets of the academy, who were seen as rigidly formal and genteelly correct. The *war of the anthologies* took place during the 1960s, when various collections of poems by both camps were published, and all the poets in the United States were required to declare their allegiance to one camp or the other or be branded as either drug addicts and perverts (by the academics) or war-mongering members of the "military-industrial complex," a term that had been coined by President Dwight D. Eisenhower in the previous decade. The onset of the Vietnam War caused the *academic poets* to abdicate their responsibilities as teachers and to join the ranks of the anti-intellectuals so that their students would not perceive them as uncaring reactionaries, a situation that caused great damage to the education of poets for decades.

The *deep image surrealism* of the Postmodernist Robert Bly (although the term was invented by the *Black Mountain* poet Amiri Baraka, born LeRoi Jones) was a late development of Imagism.

Until the rise of *the New Formalism* in the 1990s, the *experimentalism* of the 1950s was carried on into the 1990s by a school of writers calling themselves, after the periodical they established, the L=A=N=G=U=A=G=E Poets. A late-twentieth-century development of Realism was *Minimalism,* which operated on the theory that "less is enough." Narration was laconic, the dialogue often flat and without evident point, the stories anticlimactic. An example from Bret Easton Ellis's appropriately titled novel *Less Than Zero* is this passage, which begins with *summary dialogue*:

I drive to Trent's house, but Trent isn't there so I sit in his room and put a movie in the Betamax and call Blair and ask her if she wants to do something tonight, go to a club or see a movie and she says she would and I start to draw on a piece of paper that's next to the phone, recopying phone numbers on it.

"Julian wants to see you," Blair tells me.

"Yeah, I heard. Did he say what for?"

"I don't know what he wants to see you about. He just said he has to talk to you."

"Do you have his number?" I ask.

"No."

CHAPTER GLOSSARY
Italicized terms are glossed elsewhere in the book; see index.

BELLES LETTRES. Writing for literature's sake, not for a particular purpose.

BELLES-LETTRIST. One who writes without a didactic purpose. Not a hack, someone who will write anything at all for money, like the *ghost writer*, who writes something for another person to put his or her name to as the purported author.

DILETTANTE. One who dabbles in literature or various of the arts.

DOGGERELIST. See *poetaster.*

INVOCATION. In a poem, a plea for aid, generally in writing the poem, addressed to a muse, a god, or a spirit; an introductory invocation or a preface is a proem, and a prelude is an introductory poem. See Phillis Wheatley's "An Hymn to the Morning" in our companion volume, *The Book of Forms.*

LITTERATEUR. A writer who is adept in several genres or one who devotes himself or herself to literature in general.

MAN OF LETTERS. See *litterateur*.

NATURAL SYMBOL. See *symbolism*.
NOUVELLE. See *novel*.

POETASTER. A dabbler in poetry, a versifier, one who writes in verse but is incapable of rising to the level of the artist, or a *dog-gerelist*, one who writes the crudest sort of verse.
PREFACE, PRELUDE, PROEM. See *invocation*.
PRIVATE SYMBOL. See *symbolism*.

RECIT. A long story; see *novel*.

SYMBOLISM, SYMBOLS. A natural symbol holds within itself an aspect of what it symbolizes; for instance, the spider, which symbolizes death. A private symbol is one invented by a particular author; unless its significance is made clear, it may be obscure rather than illuminating. See also *signs*, in text.

VERSIFIER. See *poetaster*.

WOMAN OF LETTERS. See *litterateur*.

The Genres of Fiction

The study and theory of narration is called *narratology*. *Narratives* can emphasize any one of the four basic elements of fiction: *plot*, *character*, *atmosphere* (which includes *mood* and *setting*), or *theme* or any combination of the four, depending on how much space is available for development of any, all, or a combination of some of these elements. A narrative that emphasizes plot is a *complication story*; one that stresses character is a *character sketch*; one stressing atmosphere is a *mood piece*, relying on *ambience*; and a short narrative that relies primarily on theme is a *thematic story*.

The Dramatic Situation

The quality of *pathos* in a work of literature arouses in the reader feelings of *sympathy* or pity for the leading character, or *protagonist*. *Empathy* (German, *Einfühlung*) is a stronger emotion than sympathy, a state of identification of oneself with a character or even with an animate or inanimate object; the reader puts himself or herself in the place of the character or creature.

In fiction, *conflict* and *problem* are at the root of any *dramatic situation*, and generally speaking, a dramatic situation is the basis for all storytelling. Furthermore, it is *human conflict* in which the reader is interested, and that holds true even if the protagonist is an animal—a bird, an insect, or any other sort of creature—for that creature will display human *characteristics* with which the reader or listener will sympathize or empathize.

Narrative Structure

Plot

Plot concerns the *series of events* that take place in the narrative and the *resolution* of the conflict between protagonist and antagonist. Just as theme is the thread of thought that binds all elements of the narrative together, plot can be defined as the *thread of actions* that carries the story and serves to exemplify the theme.

The *complication story* emphasizes plot. Often a complication story will involve a *subplot,* or *secondary story line,* that runs parallel to the *main narrative*, particularly in longer narratives. The *subplot* (*minor plot* or *counterplot*) generally involves *secondary characters* of the narrative, and the actions of these characters serve to complicate or impede the main action. Often the protagonist will have to deal with the subplot's impediments before he or she can go on to deal with the main conflict, hence the term "complication" for a narrative that emphasizes plot and action. The *framework story* is a "story-within-story," and it is one structural method by which a narrative may be complicated.

An example of a novel with a double plot is *Middlemarch* by George Eliot. One plot concerns the story of Dorothea Brooke, who marries twice; the other has to do with the deeds of Dr. Ludgate and the Vincy family. It would be difficult to say which of these stories is the major one, for they are seemingly equally important; and although they are apparently separate, they are not actually so, for the one bears upon the other at critical junctures.

Another novel that more clearly has one major story and a subplot or, to be more accurate, a series of subplots, is *Great Expectations* by Charles Dickens. The protagonist is Pip, but an important secondary character is Estella, the adopted niece of Miss Havisham who has been raised to hate men in order to avenge Miss Havisham's having been jilted on her wedding night. Pip's expectations of being a gentleman seem at first to be dashed, but then he receives an inheritance from an unknown source that ultimately is found to be Abel Magwitch, a convict whom Pip had helped in earlier years, the father of Estelle. All these problems and situations and many others have to be worked out before there can be a happy ending.

Most complication stories will contain such features, beginning with the *initiating action* (*inciting moment*): the story begins at a crucial point in the plot, often *in medias res*, "in the center of things"; that is, in the center of the main action.

The first sentence of the narrative is the *narrative hook,* which is intended to create the *opening single effect,* capture the reader's attention, and pull him or her into the tale being told. Ideally, the narrative hook should give brief partial answers to as many of these questions as possible: *who? what? when? where? how?* A classic example of the narrative hook is from the short story "A Dill Pickle" by Katherine Mansfield (1888–1923): "And then, after six years, she saw him again." In nine brief words the reader is plunged into the center of the main action and knows, first, that two people are concerned, a woman and a man; second, that there had been a relationship between them at one time; third, that since then half a dozen years had passed, and finally, that they are going to reopen the book of their acquaintance. The reader's curiosity is whetted, and one wishes to know what is going to happen next.

The story then offers the reader *exposition,* bringing him or her up to the *inciting moment,* providing necessary background information and expanded answers to the questions listed above; but exposition should never overshadow action, for it is essentially static. A special sort of exposition is *foreshadowing,* giving a hint of what is to come in the story, a presentiment or premonition.

The body of the narrative is a series of *rising actions* or increasingly stronger attempts on the part of the protagonist to achieve the desired *goal.* These actions begin with the *exciting force,* which gives rise to the *inciting moment* or *defining event,* at which point the nature of the conflict between protagonist and antagonist is made clear. Each successive action culminates in a *crisis,* or *critical moment,* when protagonist and antagonist are pitted against one another. In each attempt the protagonist either fails or only partially succeeds. At some point in the story the protagonist will understand her or his situation completely, passing from "ignorance" to "knowledge" at the *moment of discovery* or *recognition,* which may mean literally recognizing the true face of the enemy. In time the series of rising actions leads to an *ultimate crisis,* the *climax,* when protagonist and antagonist are pitted against one another in a final effort. At this point the protagonist either overcomes the antagonist and achieves the goal or the conflict is lost. The *black moment* is the point in the climax when things look darkest for the chances of the protagonist. The climax in some stories is followed by the *falling action,* the *denouement (lysis)* or *unraveling* of the plot, in which all actions reach their *resolution* and the narrative is completed. The beginning of the falling action is the *tragic force* or ending of the *climactic event,* and what follows may be a *relief scene,* meant to alleviate the tension created by the plot.

The *conclusion* of the story leaves the reader with a *dominant impression,* and it is either *open* or *closed*: all loose ends are tied up neatly, or the story ends ambiguously—the actions may have been resolved but not necessarily the attitudes of the narrator, the author, or the reader. There are several ways to conclude a story: with a *hanging ending*—many modern narratives are open-ended; they are *inclusive*—with a *surprise, twist* or *trick ending,* or with a *circle-back,* in which the last sentence of the story harks back to the opening paragraph; traditional narratives are often closed; they are *exclusive*.

ANALYSIS OF WILLIAM FAULKNER'S "A ROSE FOR EMILY"

The *narrator* of William Faulkner's "A Rose for Emily" is not the author; it is a citizen of the southern town in which Miss Emily has lived her whole life. Since this is *fiction,* not *autobiography,* the reader may not assume the author was *in fact* a citizen of the town except, of course, imaginatively; thus, the *orientation* of the narration is *character orientation*. In this case the *character* is a *minor one*, a mere observer of the actions. The narrator is not talking about himself; he is talking about Miss Emily and the actions and incidents that took place during her life and afterward; therefore, it is *third-person narration*. Furthermore, Miss Emily is not the only character whose actions and incidents are narrated; rather, the narrator tells the reader about the events and people that revolved around the *protagonist*. But certain things are hidden even from the narrator until the very end of the story, so the *angle* of the story is *multiple-angle*, **not** *single-angle* nor *omnipresent-angle*. Finally, the story is told at a distance. The reader is not allowed into the minds of the characters except by *implications* generated by their *actions*. Hence, the narrator has only *objective access* to his characters. The *viewpoint (point of view)*, then, is *minor-character-oriented, third-person, multiple-angled, objective* narration.

Miss Emily is the *protagonist*, and Homer Barron seems to be the *antagonist*, except that he never really enters the story. All his actions have taken place in the past. The past is a very important factor in this story, as is the present. In fact, the time of the story is the present, but the events of the main action are told in *flashback*, that is, *dramatic exposition*, working up to the present at the conclusion of the tale, where past and present merge. Even Miss Emily is dead already as the story begins.

Miss Emily's *desire* appears to have been to be left alone to live in the past, which was the late nineteenth century. Somehow during her life she has managed to stave off the twentieth century. Even her house, in a once fine southern neighborhood, stands in the first two paragraphs as a solitary bastion encroached upon by "garages and cotton gins . . . lifting its stubborn and coquettish decay above the cotton wagons and the gasoline pumps—an eyesore among eyesores." The reader recognizes this atmospheric description as metaphorically Miss Emily herself. Standing in the way of the elderly woman's desire are time and progress—the younger generation. "Alive, Miss Emily had been a tradition, a duty, and a care; a sort of hereditary obligation on the town, . . .

When the next generation, with its more modern ideas, became mayors and aldermen," the special remission of Miss Emily's taxes, set up at the end of the nineteenth century, "created some little dissatisfaction."

This situation leads to the first *rising action*, the confrontation of Miss Emily, as a *symbol* of the decayed past, with modernity as symbolized by the new powers. The *main conflict* is a *conflict of generations*. The old is dying hard as the story opens, but it easily vanquishes the new in an initial test of strength. Miss Emily will not come to the town fathers, so they must go to her, confront her on her own ground, in all the classical decadence of what has come to be called *Southern Gothic*. The deputation of town officials mumbles to silence in the parlor filled with dust and a "crayon portrait of Miss Emily's father." In the stillness they hear the slow passage of time, "the invisible watch ticking at the end of the gold chain." Miss Emily, looking like a bloated corpse, orders Tobe, her Negro servant, himself a representative of a no longer viable past, to show the men out. "So she vanquished them, horse and foot, just as she had vanquished their fathers thirty years before about the smell."

With this sentence the reader is led into the true past and thereby into another manifestation of the conflict. This was the third time that Miss Emily stood against the town. Already, even here, the main conflict is over, that which took place between Miss Emily and Homer Barron, the Yankee engineer who had been her lover and who had deserted her. The townspeople had not cared for a peculiar smell, as of something decaying, that emanated from Miss Emily's house shortly after Homer Barron disappeared. But the townsfolk did not, on this occasion, dare to confront Miss Emily, so they sneaked into her cellar and outbuildings to sprinkle lime over everything. "After a week or two the smell went away."

At this point begins the major *exposition* of past events leading up to the death of Miss Emily's father two years earlier. Slowly, carefully, Faulkner leads the reader deeper and deeper into the past, like peeling an onion layer by layer. An incident is planted, a *foreshadowing* that hints at the story's *climax*, but subtly so that one does not see its significance until the end of the story: Miss Emily, utterly refusing to accept change, meets a delegation of grievers at the door after her father has died and insists that her father is not dead. "She did that for three days, with the ministers calling on her, and the doctors, trying to persuade her to let them dispose of the body." On this first occasion of confrontation with the town, "Just as they were about to resort to law," Miss Emily "broke down, and they buried her father quickly." Miss Emily, not yet used to being on her own in her battle to stop time, lost this first fight, but she would not lose another.

When next the reader sees the protagonist, she has become younger, to all appearances. Homer Barron (notice the *characterization by nomenclature*)—a foreigner, a modern man, a representative of change and new ways—appears for the first time, keeping company with this southern belle. Now, other *complications* ensue. Miss Emily is censured by the townsfolk for keeping company with this interloper from the North, this man of no "quality." But Miss Emily carries off the situation haughtily. Evidently, during her illness after the death of her father, she had decided (like Mr. Schaeffer in the Capote story discussed below) to be alive and young, to live now, in the present; and Homer is very much of the present. No one, including the narrator, knows much about him; however, the reader does not get close to him as a solid personality. Emily knew him quite well, though, and soon rumors were flying. Still, Miss Emily "carried her head high enough—even when we believed that she was fallen." Almost incidentally, at this point, Miss Emily buys some rat poison.

Evidently, there has been personal conflict going on between Miss Emily and her lover. The townsfolk—who have operated throughout the story like the *chorus* of a Greek *tragedy*, commenting on actions that take place *offstage*, behind the scenes—fear suicide. Perhaps, considering her disgrace, "it would be the best thing," for "she will marry him" had been changed to "she will persuade him yet," though Homer had made it known that "he was not a marrying man."

Again the townspeople become indignant: "it was a disgrace to the town and a bad example to the young people." They force a minister to confront her in this second battle of wills, but he is evidently routed so badly he will neither speak of what happened nor return to the house. So the folk write to her relatives, and some of them come to Miss Emily to help bring things to a head. "At first nothing happened," but at last it seems as though Emily and Homer are married, which is a great relief to the neighbors. Miss Emily orders "a man's toilet set in silver, with the letters H. B. on each piece." She buys a man's outfit. The cousins had done their work. "So we were not surprised when Homer Barron . . . was gone." "[W]e believed that he had gone on to prepare for Miss Emily's coming, or to give her a chance to get rid of the cousins." Eventually, the cousins leave, and Homer reappears. In the light of later events the reader assumes that Barron has delivered an ultimatum offstage: "The cousins or me, and no marriage under any circumstances."

Homer is not seen again, and as time passes, Miss Emily quickly grows old. Her door is kept closed; the smell is ancient history. Only Tobe is allowed in or out, except during a period of several years during which Miss Emily taught china painting to "daughters and granddaughters" of the older generation, each of whom brought a "donation," for Miss Emily couldn't work for a living any more than she could accept "charity."

"Then the newer generation became the backbone and the spirit of the town, and the painting pupils fell away and did not send their children." Miss Emily, Tobe, and the house grow older and more decayed; the neighborhood and town change, becoming modern. Thus, Miss Emily "passed from generation to generation—dear, inescapable, impervious, tranquil and perverse."

"And so she died." And as at last the representatives of a new age appear on the doorstep, Tobe opens the portal and vanishes. The cousins reappear; the funeral is held. The very old men come wearing Confederate uniforms, talk of Miss Emily "as if she had been a contemporary of theirs, believing they had danced with her and courted her perhaps, confusing time with its mathematical progression, as the old do, to whom all the past is not a diminishing road, but, instead, a huge meadow which no winter ever quite touches, divided from them now by the narrow bottleneck of the most recent decade of years." And the *structure* of the story, its *architectonics*, has mirrored this confusion and bottleneck of time.

In that meadow, in the bed in the sealed-off room upstairs, which the townsfolk were careful to leave closed until Miss Emily was decently underground, there lay the decayed corpse of love, of youth, of the harbinger of change and new ways, in "the attitude of an embrace." The reader is given to understand that Miss Emily had continued to lie with Homer Barron on their "wedding" bed but that living flesh was no more capable of withstanding decay than dead flesh and that at last even Miss Emily had to succumb to the ravages of generations and time.

Character

The only *person* absolutely necessary in a story is the *protagonist*, a *main character* or *hero/heroine*, although these latter terms, derived from classical *drama* (q.v.), really have more specialized meanings. In modern fiction and drama the protagonist sometimes exhibits the opposite of the characteristics of a hero; such a *persona* is called an *antihero*, like Yossarian in Joseph Heller's novel *Catch-22*. This term is not to be confused with *antagonist*, which is a *character*, *force*, or *circumstance* that stands in opposition to the protagonist. A narrative can have a *multiple protagonist*—a group or village, for instance, as in Shirley Jackson's short story "The Lottery"—though normally one person will represent such a *composite protagonist*. A *naive hero* is a protagonist who is so simple or honest that his view of what occurs in the narrative is obviously wrong or misguided to the *audience* or the *reader*; Cervantes' Don Quixote is a naive hero. Other *personae* or even the *narrator* of a story or play may be naive as well.

The protagonist possesses a *desire* to have, to be, or to do something (there are no other options). This desire will drive the protagonist toward an *objective* or *goal*, but attainment of the goal will be blocked by an antagonist. The *opposition* of protagonist versus antagonist leads to *conflict*, which is essential to the *dramatic situation*.

The antagonist is often another person in logical opposition, but it need not be a human being; it may be a *situation* (being lost in a blizzard), a *force* (society, a corporation), or oneself (an *inner conflict*). If one is lost in a blizzard and one's desire is to reach shelter and be saved, the force of the storm is the antagonist. If one is unhappily married but there are children, one may be torn between a desire for happiness, or at least relief from misery, and duty to others. In such a case the antagonist is oneself, and the conflict is an *inner conflict*. This is the classic *formula* for fiction: desire, opposition, conflict.

In a story of any size, the conflict must be prolonged over the *duration* of the *narrative*, which means that protagonist and antagonist must be evenly matched and the narrative ends only when the protagonist achieves his or her desire or fails to achieve it. Besides his or her desire, a protagonist has a *dominant personality trait*, such as courage, generosity, or fervor. However, a character should never be so consistent as to be ruled absolutely by this dominant trait, for real human beings are complex because they have traits that often contradict one another. Therefore, a protagonist ought to have at least one *countertrait* that renders him or her not entirely predictable.

For instance, a dominant personality trait in a character might be courage; a countertrait might be a fear of heights. If, in a given situation, the character must display courage while he is on a rooftop, the countertrait will throw the protagonist's response to danger into question. *Character* (in the sense of *moral character*) has to do with these *personality features* of the persons in the narrative. Such personal characteristics determine the *actions* and *reactions* of the persons in the story. A character will have other *traits* and *characteristics* as well, including the physical—eye, hair and skin coloration, body build, a nervous tic, a particular manner of speaking, and so forth. All of these characteristics should blend in such a manner as to make the persona interesting, to give him or her individuality.

A modern *well-made story* must ordinarily be "truer to life than life." In most narratives, therefore, there can be no *coincidences* that are important to the struggle of the protagonist with the antagonist, for the protagonist must solve his or her own problems.

Aside from the protagonist and antagonist, there may be other sorts of characters in a story, including a *foil,* who is a persona that serves a particular purpose in the narrative. A foil is often a *sidekick,* a companion who sometimes gives the protagonist important information or insights, often accidentally, as Dr. Watson does in the Sherlock Holmes stories of Arthur Conan Doyle or as Captain Hastings does in the Hercule Poirot stories of Agatha Christie. A *confidant* (feminine, *confidante*) is a minor character or foil who acts as a *sounding board* for one of the major characters, often the heroine.

Characterization is the depiction of personality in fiction. The best means of characterization is through *action*; the second best is through *dialogue*. Other means of characterization are through the dialogue and actions/reactions of other characters in the story, and it is also possible to use characterization by nomenclature (see above). A *hero* may be named, perhaps, Sherlock Holmes, but his *sidekick* might best be named Dr. Watson, and the *villain* of the piece would aptly be named Professor Moriarty. A *static* or *flat character* is a persona with only a surface, no depth; in other words, a *stereotype*. A *round character* is one that is filled out, that is believable as the characterization of a real person.

Interactive dialogue is dialogue seen in actions. One character may be speaking, but another may say nothing, merely reacting to what is being said, as in this passage from Agatha Christie's *The Pale Horse*:

What the quarrel was about, apart from terms of abuse, I did not gather. Cries and catcalls arose from other tables.

"Attagirl! Sock her, Lou!"

The proprietor behind the bar, a slim Italian-looking fellow with sideburns, whom I had taken to be Luigi, came to intervene in a voice that was pure cockney London.

"Nah then—break it up—You'll 'ave the whole street in in a minute. You'll 'ave the coppers here. Stop it, I say."

But the lanky blonde had the redhead by the hair and was tugging furiously as she screamed:

"You're nothing but a man-stealing witch!"

"Witch yourself."

Luigi and the two embarrassed escorts forced the girls apart. In the blonde's fingers were large tufts of red hair. She held them aloft gleefully, then dropped them on the floor.

The door from the street was pushed open and Authority, dressed in blue, stood on the threshold and uttered the regulation words majestically.

"What's going on here?"

"Just a bit of fun," said one of the young men.

"That's all," said Luigi. "Just a bit of fun among friends."

With his foot he kicked the tufts of hair adroitly under the nearest table. The contestants smiled at each other in false amnesty.

The policeman looked at everybody suspiciously.

Atmosphere

Atmosphere is the *mood* of the narrative, and mood is created by means of *setting* (*locale* and surroundings in which the narrative takes place), *attitude* (of the narrator and of the characters in the narrative), and *descriptions*. Though atmosphere and setting are connected, they may be considered separately to a degree. The setting of a story is the *location* or locations in which the story takes place. Setting is to written narrative what a *set* is to a *play*. The *exposition* (or *antecedent action*) of a story is its *background*, which is to be distinguished from its setting.

Atmosphere is the *aura* of mood that surrounds the story. It is to fiction what the *sensory level* is to poetry. In fact, it is often said that a story that has as its strongest element a mood or atmosphere is a *"poetic" story*. Such narratives were perhaps more popular in the past, especially in the *Gothic fiction* of the nineteenth century, than they are in the twentieth century. Gothic literature emphasizes the enigmatic, the dark, the distorted: the stories of Nathaniel Hawthorne and Edgar Allan Poe were often Gothic stories.

The mood story attempts by *descriptions* and *emotive means* to influence the perceptions of the reader, to call into play *sensations* and *emotions*. The setting of the story will have a great deal to do with these *evocations* of mood. What would a ghost story be without an old Victorian mansion with creaking doors, an ancient castle full of cobwebs, or some other such *Gothic setting*? This is not to suggest that an author might not write a ghost story about a primrose cottage, merely that such a setting would be unusual and untraditional, and the writer would have to do certain things to compensate for these missing elements of the Gothic. Even more important than setting, however, is the manner in which characters, actions, and locations are described. These ways are often *metaphorical*, as in poetry: The descriptions are heightened through *simile* and *metaphor*.

ANALYSIS OF TRUMAN CAPOTE'S "A DIAMOND GUITAR"

Truman Capote's short story "A Diamond Guitar" is about men in prison where there is a great deal of time for reflection. Capote puts the emphasis upon such constructions as these: "and at night with the pines waving frostily and a freezing light falling from the moon"; "He stood there whispering the names of the evening stars as they opened in flower above him. The stars were his pleasure, but tonight they did not comfort him; they did not make him remember what happens to us on earth is lost in the endless shine of eternity"; "To be alive was to remember brown rivers where the fish run, and sunlight on a lady's hair"; "Of the seasons of the year, spring is the most shattering; stalks thrusting through the earth's winter-stiffened crust, young leaves cracking out on old left-to-die branches, the falling-asleep wind cruising through all the newborn green."

Heightened language operates on more than one level. Taking this last quotation as an example, one may see that, on the surface—on the *narrative level*—the *descriptions* are of spring, and they help the reader to sense the season, which is part of the *setting*. Many readers, at least on a conscious level, may let it go at this, but it is not only the season Capote is describing. The passage is also a *metaphorical depiction* of Capote's *protagonist*, the elderly prisoner named Mr. Schaeffer. Tico Feo, a young man and a new fellow prisoner, has come like spring to waken Mr. Schaeffer out of the winter sleep into which he has fallen since he has been incarcerated. This "sleep" has been protective. The crust of winter has kept dreams of life from bursting through the surface, "shattering" his deliberately inculcated composure, his "contentment" with prison life.

But now, like an old tree, Mr. Shaeffer has been wakened to life when it is too late ever to be young again. Nevertheless, he begins to hope, to put forth "newborn green" leaves. The "left-to-die" branches unwillingly begin to stir in the spring of a new awareness. Yet Mr. Schaeffer must know that this hope is deceptive. He can never be again as Tico Feo is, young and "free," at least in his mind and in his expectations. Capote's protagonist is driven, despite this knowledge, to enter life again, to feel the blood and the sap flowing in brittle wood and bone. These images of rejuvenation are parts of a *controlling image* that help to give the story its shape and temper, its *timbre*.

Every story, whether fiction or drama, has its *background* as well. Many stories begin in the middle of the first *major action* of the *plot*, and though such a beginning is intriguing to the audience, the writer will eventually have to explain how things got to such a pass in the first place. That is its *exposition*. For instance, "A Diamond Guitar" begins *in medias res*, with Mr. Schaeffer already in prison, and Tico Feo almost immediately arrives to begin the old man's transformation. The action of the story is concerned with the prison, but both Mr. Schaeffer and Tico Feo got there somehow in the first place. Perhaps it doesn't much matter how they became prisoners as far as the plot is concerned, but it does matter as far as logic and *reader interest* are concerned.

The reader is therefore given, as the story progresses, certain information about the backgrounds of the two main characters. At this point one might notice that, though Tico Feo is a sympathetic character, he is nevertheless the *antagonist*, because it is he who causes Mr. Schaeffer to come into conflict with his situation; this is an example of *conflict without enmity*. The reader is given to understand that Mr. Schaeffer is an essentially good man who committed only one "truly bad" act in his life—he killed a man. Although the man "deserved to die," Mr. Schaeffer had to pay the price of his deed. Likewise, Tico Feo was sent to prison because he was involved in a knifing. He killed no one, so his sentence is short. Even so, he can't wait two years, and he plans to escape. This exposition serves two purposes here: first, it satisfies the reader's curiosity as to how these men got to prison; second, it helps to characterize them.

Theme

Theme is the thread of *idea* that underlies the story. All narrative elements support the theme, which must be distinguished from the *subject*. The subject of a narrative can be expressed in a *word* or *phrase*, but the theme is always expressible only in a *complete sentence*: Death may be a subject, but what one says about death is the theme, which may be expressed perhaps in the sentence "Each time a friend dies, a bit of oneself dies as well." Stories ought not to *moralize*—overemphasize the theme.

A term closely related to theme is *leitmotif* or *motif*, which are ideational elements that recur from time to time throughout a literary or other artistic work, such as a musical composition. Some standard motifs are the *ubi sunt* (where are they now?), the similar *ou sont les neiges d'antan* (where are the snows of yesteryear?), the *carpe diem* (seize the day), the *contemptus mundi* (the real world is beneath contempt), and the *mea culpa* (I am guilty), a staple of the *confessional literature* genre.

Voice

Someone speaks in every poem, story, and essay ever written. Thus, there are three *narrative viewpoints,* which parallel the three major and traditional *syntaxes*—the *subjective*, the *narrative*, and the *dramatic* voices—and there are other considerations as well. The first is **orientation**. In the *author-oriented viewpoint* the author narrates the story, either the real author or the *putative author*, that is, the supposed author of the narration, as in *Gulliver's Travels* by Jonathan Swift, the putative author of which is "Lemuel Gulliver," not Swift himself. In the *character-oriented viewpoint* a character in the story narrates, either a *major character* (protagonist or antagonist) or a *minor character*.

Person is the next consideration. The story can be narrated in the *first person singular* ("I saw what happened") or possibly *first person plural* ("We saw what happened"). It also can be narrated in the *second person singular* or possibly *second person plural* ("You saw what happened"). Finally, the story can be told in the *third person singular* ("He [she, it] saw what happened") or plural ("They saw what happened").

The third consideration is **perspective**. From the *single perspective*, only the actions of one character are followed; only what occurs in that character's presence is narrated. From the *multiple perspective* (double, triple, etc.) what occurs in the presence of two or more characters is narrated. From the *omnipresent perspective* the narrator has access to actions everywhere in the story.

Access is the fourth consideration. The narrator might have only *objective access* to occurrences, being able to narrate only actions seen or heard, or the narrator might have *subjective access*, being able to narrate not only actions and words but the thoughts and emotions of characters as well.

As with all other elements, the author can blend any combination of orientation, person, access, and perspective. The *omniscient viewpoint* is a combination of author-oriented, third-person, and omnipresent-perspective narration with subjective access. In other words, the narrator knows all about everything, internal and external, everywhere in the story, and narrates it thus. It is important that any writer figure out all the ramifications of the narrative viewpoint chosen before the story is written; otherwise, he or she may have to switch viewpoints in mid-tale, and that will destroy the reader's *willing suspension of disbelief* (see the *unities,* described in the following chapter).

Aspects of Narration

These have to do with the *stance,* the *tone,* of the narrator, whether he or she tells the story in a particular manner—so as to make the reader laugh (*the humorous stance*) or cry (the *melodramatic* or *tragic* or *melancholy* or *reflective* stance). *Tone* is a distinctive quality of expression or *intonation,* as in "tone of voice." There are as many stances as there are emotions to be evoked, and as many tones of voice as there are types of people in the world. Certainly, the author who chose to have his narrator tell the story from a melancholy stance would consider the tale a failure if it evoked laughter. It would, however, be possible to choose a serious narrator who evokes laughter by means of *dramatic irony,* which is an effect produced when the audience knows more about the character and the character's situation than the character does. *Romantic irony* has the author-narrator of a story stepping back from his creation and discussing it with an air of detachment, thus displaying to the reader that he or she is actually uninvolved with and free from the predicaments of the personae of the narrative. In the twentieth century this sort of narration would be considered *authorial intrusion,* roiling the waters of the still pond of *mimesis* or "imitation of reality" unless, of course, the novelist were writing *black humor,* as in the novel *Catch 22* by Joseph Heller, who juxtaposes macabre elements with realistic ones and ridiculous situations with terrifying occurrences; or in novels by such *metafiction* writers as John Barth, whose works, like the story "Lost in the Funhouse," often discuss the creation of fiction at the same time that the fiction is being created.

The *frame narrative* employs what amounts to a *double narrator,* for it is a *story within a story*. Joseph Conrad begins his novel *Heart of Darkness* this way:

The *Nellie,* a cruising yawl, swung to her anchor without a flutter of the sails, and was at rest.

It would appear at first that this is *author-oriented narration,* but Conrad continues:

The Director of Companies was our captain and our host. We four affectionately watched his back as he stood in the bows looking to seaward.

The Lawyer—the best of old fellows—had, because of his many years and many virtues, the only cushion on deck, and was lying on the only rug. The Accountant had brought out already a box of dominoes, and was toying architecturally with the bones. Marlow sat cross-legged right aft, leaning against the mizzen-mast. He had sunken cheeks, a yellow complexion, a straight back, an ascetic aspect, and, with his arms dropped, the palms of hands outwards, resembled an idol.

It thus becomes apparent that the narrator is not the author; one of the characters aboard the *Nellie* is. It is not Marlow, who will be the *protagonist* of the story, although somewhat later that character will appear to be someone named *Kurtz*. After some scene-setting and atmosphere painting,

"And this also," said Marlow suddenly, "has been one of the dark places of the earth."

It is at this point that the narrative begins, and Marlow takes up the narration as the *frame narrator* of the novel. The narration of the novel is basically a *monologue* by Marlow; his audience is not the audience reading the book but the four people on the deck of the *Nellie*, one of whom was the original narrator of the story, which is *minor-character-oriented, third-person, single-perspective, objective-access narration*. Now and again, Conrad will remind the reader of this fact by recalling the original narrator of the story.

Conrad does not thus commit *author intrusion*; that occurs when, the *dramatic illusion* having been established through the reader's *willing suspension of disbelief*, the author does something that calls attention to himself, thereby breaking the spell of the story. For instance, in his novel *Falconer*, John Cheever establishes that the narration will be author-oriented, third-person, **single-perspective**, subjective narration. His protagonist is in prison. All goes well until Cheever comes to a spot in the plot where the narration needs to leave the physical bounds of the prison. That means that the author must awkwardly shift the viewpoint of the story because, his prisoner being unable to leave the prison, the perspective must suddenly be doubled to tell the story of a second person. Cheever has abruptly changed the terms of the narration he established and called himself to the attention of the reader, breaking the reader's concentration on the story.

Another sort of author intrusion is *editorializing*, the author stepping forward and taking a position on the story being related. Over the years since the eighteenth century this convention has grown less and less acceptable, but it does occur in twentieth-century *metafiction*.

Motivation

It is the purpose of nearly all literature to convince the audience that the author's insight is valid. For example, in a poem, even if the poet writes merely to sing a song of joy, nothing more, the poet will fail unless he or she convinces the reader that the joy expressed in the poem is a true joy. Equally, the story writer will fail to convince if the elements of the story do not support the theme. For instance, assume that an author has written a story on the theme "All men are corruptible." Assume, too, that to prove this point the author chooses as his characters a loan shark, a politician, a drug addict, and a coward. Will the story be likely to convince the reader of man's essentially corruptible nature? If the author instead chooses a suburban housewife, a priest, a teacher, and a doctor, what will happen? The difference between these two groups is that the second is much more representative of mankind in general and will tend to support the theme better than the first group, which may be more easily seen as atypical and thus more susceptible to corruption.

The characters of a story must act in accordance with their personality traits if their actions are to be believable. If the protagonist of a particular story has the dominant trait of bravery and the author's theme is that all people feel fear at times, in a dangerous situation it is believable that the protagonist will feel afraid but will act bravely anyway. If, however, the brave person turns and runs when she or he feels fear, the theme will tend to be disproved unless, of course, the protagonist gets a second chance and thus proves that she or he is brave after all.

CHAPTER GLOSSARY
Italicized terms are glossed elsewhere in the book; see index.

ACTION FICTION. The genre that includes spy novels, adventure stories, tales of intrigue ("cloak and dagger") and terror, mysteries—that is, detective stories or tales of ratiocination, as they were called by Edgar Allan Poe (1809–49), inventor of the form, a specimen of which is "The Murders in the Rue Morgue." These kinds of stories utilize *suspense*, the *tension*—a *balance* created between opposing principles, situations, or techniques—that is built up when the reader wishes to know how the conflict between the protagonist and antagonist is going to be resolved or what the solution to the puzzle of a thriller is.

ADAPTATION. Transformation of one sort of thing into another through transcription, for instance, turning a novel into a *screenplay*. However, the opposite also is possible: to novelize is to turn a screenplay into a novel.

ADVENTURE STORIES. See *action fiction*.

ANIMAL STORIES. See *children's literature*.

ANTINOVEL. A work that denies the traditional structure of the novel; proceeds without plot, character, atmosphere, or even theme; and is presented as a series of fragments from which the reader is to construct her or his own "novel."

ANTIREALISM. Fiction of the absurd—see discussion of *theater of the absurd* in text, and *metafiction*. Although the antirealist novel and the antinovel would appear to be synonyms, in fact the two camps reject one another on theoretical grounds. James Joyce and Franz Kafka are counted as two antirealist novelists, though the former is considered a stream-of-consciousness writer and the latter is counted a surrealist.

APPRENTICESHIP NOVEL. See *bildungsroman*.

AUTHORIAL INTRUSION. See *dialogue*.

BACKWOODS BOAST. A tirade out of America's pioneering days, but the brag is an English tradition as old as *Beowulf*.

> I'm the biggest, baddest bald-headed bear this side of the Pecos. I can eat a pony and a side of rhinoceros with one ear and holler out of the other one. I can fit a bayou in my left cheek and whistle Dixie too, and when I do, you know Dixie's gonna come with a ring-tailed raccoon chewin' on her heels, and it ain't gonna take her no ten minutes neither, no-how. You wanta know my name? Why, you couldn't fit it in a six-volume 'cyclopedia, it's so long! I'll tell you what—just call me whatever you like and I'll answer, long as there's a gallon of moon involved, but don't call me Fred, 'cause I ain't a Fred of any man.

BATHOS. Failed or banal pathos, the depths of sentimentality (as distinguished from sentiment), the opposite of hypsos, the height of emotion. See discussion of the pathetic fallacy in *The Book of Forms*.

BILDUNGSROMAN. An apprenticeship novel that shows the development and civilizing of a young person as he or she matures, like the *Künstlerroman,* which is specifically about the development of an artist, as in James Joyce's *A Portrait of the Artist as a Young Man.*

BRAG. See *backwoods boast*.

CARTOON. See *children's literature*.

CHARACTER ROLES. Seven character roles have been isolated in fairy tales: the seeker or victim, who is the protagonist; the *villain*, the antagonist; the sought, who has been lost or captured, often a princess; the dispatcher, who sends the seeker on his quest; the donor, the helper, and the false hero. Sometimes one character may fulfill two or more roles in a particular story; likewise, one role may be played by more than two characters. A refined version of this cast is the actantial model: the subject, who seeks the object; the object, who is sought by the subject; the sender, who dispatches the subject on his or her quest; the receiver, who is the recipient of the object; the helper (or sidekick) of the subject; and the opponent who is, of course, the antagonist.

CHILDREN'S LITERATURE. Includes such types as picture books, in which illustrations and words are of equal importance to the text or in which the illustrations are predominant, as they are also in the cartoon, the comic strip, and the comic book. The pop-up book is a children's volume in which the illustration, or part of it, erects itself into a three-dimensional image when the book is opened. Pictures are often an important part of the collection of nursery rhymes as well: traditional verses told often under the aegis of "Mother Goose." See our companion volume, *The New Book of Forms: A Handbook of Poetics*.

The fairy tale (German, *märchen*) is a story of fabulous incidents involving witches, goblins, giants, and such creatures. Animal stories are tales in which creatures are the primary characters or even the narrators. The *just-so story* tells children how something came to pass or to be; for instance, "How the Rabbit Grew Long Ears." A *fable* is a short moral tale that uses animals as characters, as in *Aesop's Fables*. The moral always is one that applies to human beings, however, and the animals are actually merely human beings in disguise, as in "The Ugly Duckling." A tall tale is a yarn, a lie told tongue-in-cheek, such as some of the stories of Mark Twain (1835–1910) and the Uncle Remus series of Joel Chandler Harris (1848–1908).

CLOAK AND DAGGER. See *action fiction*.

COMIC BOOK. See *children's literature*.

COMIC STRIP. See *children's literature*.

COMMERCIAL SUCCESS. See *epigone*.

CONVERSATION. See *dialogue*.

CRITICAL SUCCESS. See *epigone*.

DETECTIVE STORY. See *action fiction*.

DIALOGUE. Dialogue (*dialogismus*) is *conversation* among characters in a story, and it is used for many purposes. It is the second best technique after action to help to characterize one of the personae of the story. *Monologue* is half of a conversation, a speech to a character who is presumed to be present, though a listener may not be evident to the audience. A *soliloquy* is differentiated from a monologue in that it is personal thoughts verbalized rather than half a conversation; it is "talking to oneself," for no other audience is present or assumed to be present.

DIME NOVEL. See *pulp fiction*.

DUNGEONS AND DRAGONS. See *fantasy* and *science fiction*.

DYSTOPIA. See *utopian novel*.

EPIGONE. One who writes a lesser imitation of a literary work. In both fiction and drama, and particularly of late in cinema, the sequel is the name of the game; for trying to ride on the back of a *commercial success* by coming up with another story, and yet another, having the same characters and situations and much the same plot, is much better, in the eyes of producers, than merely achieving a *critical success* or, to give it its tonier French name, a *succès d'estime*.

EPISTOLARY NOVEL. One written in the form of letters or "epistles."

ESCAPE LITERATURE. Easy reading, meant to take the mind off one's own everyday concerns. See *science fiction, romance*.

FABLE. See *children's literature*. See also the *fabliau* in "The Genres of Poetry" in *The Book of Forms*.

FAIRY TALE. See *children's literature*.

FANTASY. Fiction about imaginary worlds or happenings; see *magic realism*, which is a current form of fantasy. See also *science fiction*.

FEMINIST FICTION. Fiction that is not merely written from the viewpoint of a woman but addresses and treats of such concerns as women's problems in a paternalist society; self-fulfillment in other than traditional ways, such as childbearing and child rearing; and the expansion of roles and activities. See also *Gaia fiction*.

FICTION OF THE ABSURD. See theater of the absurd in "The Genres of Drama" and *metafiction*.

FOLKLORE. The oral tradition of a people's passing on its myths and traditional songs and tales (*folktales*).

FOLKSONG. See *folklore, myth*. Also see folk ballad in *The Book of Forms*.

FOLKTALE. See *folklore, myth*.

FORMULA STORY. A narrative written to a set pattern. The traditional *formula story* can follow several patterns. The rags-to-riches motif has the poor, hardworking young person rising above his or her environment to become a captain of industry or something equivalent. Boy meets girl, boy loses girl, boy gets girl is a standard formula, as is the eternal triangle love story. The Robin Hood formula has the popular hero stealing from the rich to give to the poor. See also *pulp fiction*.

GAIA FICTION. A type of current *feminist fiction* in which the central focus is Earth and Earth's relationship to characters and themes. The word "Gaia," the Greek earth goddess, resurfaced as a synonym denoting the world in James Lovelock's preface to his 1987 revised edition of *Gaia: A New Look at Life on Earth*.

GENERIC NARRATIVES. See *genre fiction* and *mythoi*.

GENRE FICTION. The term covers specialized fields of fiction other than "mainstream fiction," including adventure, mysteries, science fiction, romance, confession, children's literature, and many others that are covered in this glossary.

GHOST STORY. See *supernatural fiction*.

GOSSIP. See *novel*.

GOTHIC FICTION. Stories about dark, gloomy, brooding (the Byronic hero), and sometimes supernatural people and events. In it there is often a great deal of atmosphere, distortions of reality, desolation, and mystery. The genre began in England in the eighteenth century but achieved two of its greatest successes in the nineteenth century with Mary Wollstonecraft Shelley's novel *Frankenstein* and Bram Stoker's *Dracula*.

HISTORICAL NOVEL. See *roman à clef*.

ILLUSTRATION. A picture intended to accompany a literary text. See *children's literature*.

INTERIOR MONOLOGUE. See *dialogue*.

JUST-SO STORY. The term is from Rudyard Kipling's collection *Just-So Stories,* which includes "How the Whale Got His Throat," "How the Camel Got His Hump," and "How the Leopard Got His Spots." See *children's literature*.

JUVENILES. Stories and books written for young people in the genre of *children's literature*.

KÜNSTLERROMAN. See *bildungsroman*.

LEGEND. See *myth*.

MAGIC REALISM. Fiction in which the fantastic is treated in an ordinary way, as though it were "normal," part of everyday reality, as in the novel *One Hundred Years of Solitude* by Gabriel García Márquez.

MAINSTREAM FICTION. Non-genre fiction; that is, fiction not written in one of the subcategories of fiction, such as romances, westerns, mysteries, confessions, science fiction, and so forth.

MANNERISM. Stylistic affectation, such as the overuse of particular words, or peculiarities of writing, for instance, the overuse of *tag lines*. See *romance*.

MÄRCHEN. See *children's literature*.

METAFICTION. Fiction about fiction, as in the short story "Lost in the Funhouse" by John Barth, which is simultaneously a treatise on how to write a short story and an exploration of the metaphor that life is a house of mirrors, mishap, and magic.

MIMESIS. The imitation in literature and art of the real world; the representation of actuality in art and literature. See naturalism (in text), *realism*, and *verisimilitude*.

MONOLOG, MONOLOGUE. See *dialogue*.

MONOMYTH. See *myth*.

MOTIF. See *formula story*.

MYSTERIES. See *action fiction*.

MYTH. The oldest stories are called myths; mythology is concerned with the supernatural origins of a people and with the legendary "history" of a culture, including its theology (system of religious beliefs) and pantheon (its gods). Typically, myths were meant to explain both the natural and the supernatural worlds in a prescientific world. Northrop Frye posited four mythoi, or "generic narratives," central to the study of genre: spring, *comedy*; summer, *romance;* autumn, *tragedy*, and winter, satire. The monomyth, according to Joseph Campbell in his *Hero with a Thousand Faces*, is the central myth in a particular culture, such as the quest myth or the creation myth.

MYTHOI. See *myth*.

MYTHOLOGY. See *myth*.

MYTHOPOESIS. Conscious literary mythmaking, as in J. R. R. Tolkien's *The Lord of the Rings*. See *myth*.

NATURALISM. See *realism* and *verisimilitude*.

NOVEL. The term *novel* is derived from the Italian *novella,* meaning "news item" or "gossip." In its modern sense, a novel is a fictive tale of considerable length having all the characteristics of fiction and the space in which to develop them in detail. The original term, "novella," now is taken to mean a short novel: a narrative that is longer than a short story but shorter than a full-length novel. A *novelette* or *novelet* is a synonym for novella in most dictionaries, but experts make a distinction: the novelette is the sort of romantic *formula story* that is published singly or serialized (i.e., published in installments) in women's magazines; the *novella* is a serious work of fiction.

NOVEL OF MANNERS. Fiction that observed the sensibilities and actions of the genteel middle class in England, as in the work of Jane Austen (1775–1817).

NOVELET, NOVELETTE. See *novel*.

NOVELIZATION. See *adaptation*.

NOVELLA. See *novel*.

NURSERY RHYME. See *children's literature*. See also "The Genres of Poetry" in *The Book of Forms*.

PACE. See *movement, tag line*.

PANTHEON. See *myth*.

PARAFICTION. A term meant to indicate a type of nonfiction that is written LIKE fiction, as Truman Capote's *In Cold Blood* was written like a novel. Although such nonfiction is not itself short stories, novels, novellas, and so forth, many of the techniques used in it are those of narration, including plot, atmosphere, characterization, and theme.

PENNY DREADFUL. See *pulp fiction*.

PICARESQUE NOVEL. A novel that has as its hero a lovable rogue who wanders about having many adventures. The narrative is organized through the picaro's adventures; he is not only its protagonist but also its controlling figure.

PICARO. The protagonist of a *picaresque novel*.

PICTURE BOOKS. See *children's literature*.

POP-UP BOOK. See *children's literature*.

PROBLEM NOVEL. Also called *roman à thèse,* it explores social issues, like *Tess of the D'Urbervilles* by Thomas Hardy (1840–1928) or *Bleak House* by Charles Dickens (1812–1870). A special kind of problem novel is the proletarian novel, like the Studs Lonigan trilogy of James T. Farrell (1904–79), which examines the situation of the working class.

PROLETARIAN NOVEL. See *problem novel*.

PSEUDOAUTOBIOGRAPHIES. See *true histories*.

PULP FICTION. A category that takes its name from books published on the cheapest paper, which, in the modern era, is made from wood pulp. The earliest such volumes were called chapbooks, a corruption of "cheap books," which were sold on the streets by chapmen. The volumes published in Erastus Flavel Beadle's 1860 Dime Book series were known as dime novels. The British equivalent of the dime novel is the older penny dreadful. Contemporary pulp fiction volumes are called paperbacks or paperback novels, but since many books are published now in paperback format, a distinction is made between pulp paperbacks and "quality paperbacks."

PUNCTUATION OF DIALOGUE. See *summary dialogue*.

PURPLE PROSE. See *romance*.

REALISM. The technique of giving the impression, in writing, of the real world; see *mimesis* and *verisimilitude*.

ROMAN À CLEF. A work that has as its characters actual living people disguised as fictive personae, unlike the historical novel, which uses historical figures and situations but inserts fictive characters as well.

ROMAN À THÈSE. See *problem novel*.

ROMANCE. In the modern rather than the medieval sense, novels of sexual love between stereotypical adults set in idealized situations, usually written in purple prose—a breathless, gushy, overwritten style full of *mannerisms*, such as the overuse of adjectives. These sorts of novels are often called *escape literature* because they take readers away from the cares of the workaday world for a little while. They are also *formula stories* with plots that are virtually indistinguishable from one another.

SAGA. The saga was a medieval Icelandic prose narrative written from about 1120 to 1400. Its subject matter had to do with the first settlers of Iceland and their progeny, and it recapitulated the royal history and mythology of the Norse. Modern family stories of similar structure are also called sagas; *Buddenbrooks*, by Thomas Mann, is an example.

SCIENCE FICTION (*sci-fi*). Fiction that concerns itself with speculative events in future worlds and societies or with imaginative (sometimes prophetic) scientific and medical discoveries. Science fiction sometimes is cross-fertilized by other genres, in particular fantasy, as in the contemporary subgenres called dungeons and dragons. See also the *utopian novel*.

SCREENPLAY. See *adaptation*.

SEQUEL. See *epigone*.

SERIAL. See *novel* and *triple-decker*.

SIGNIFICATIO. The classical term for foreshadowing; hinting at what is to come.

SOLILOQUY. See *dialogue*.

SPY NOVELS. See *action fiction*.

STEREOTYPE. See *romance*.

STREAM OF CONSCIOUSNESS. A twentieth-century technique that is intended to give the impression, through interior monologue, of the way the mind actually works—wandering from digression to digression, leaping from one association to another, leaving out connectives, eliding, using disjunctive syntax, and so forth. James Joyce's *Finnegan's Wake* is an example, as is William Faulkner's *The Sound and the Fury*.

SUCCÈS D'ESTIME. See *epigone*.

SUMMARY DIALOGUE. The description of a conversation, for instance, when a character is telling his or her own story within the story: "So I said to Caroline, 'What did John say?' and she told me that **he had said he wanted to go home to his wife and children and to stop messing his life up with other women**." Sometimes this is called the panoramic method of narrative exposition. The punctuation of this passage is double quotation marks for the first conversation, single quotation marks for the conversation within the first conversation, and so forth, ad infinitum. British fiction uses quotations the other way around: first single quotes, then double, then single, and so forth. For another example of summary dialogue, see the discussion of *minimalism,* in text.

SUPERNATURAL FICTION. A genre of fiction that is concerned with ghosts and hauntings, extraordinary psychic occurrences, and so forth. It is a form of *gothic fiction*.

SUSPENSE. See *action fiction*.

TAG LINE. One or two words or a phrase that indicates to the reader who is speaking in a story: "Have you been home today?" **the policeman asked**. Too many tag lines in a story are a form of author intrusion, and they can interfere with the pace of the story, the quickness with which the action and dialogue move.

TALE. A synonym for story.

TALES OF INTRIGUE. See *action fiction*.

TALES OF RATIOCINATION. See *action fiction*.

TALES OF TERROR. See *action fiction*.

TALL TALE. A lie. Also see *children's literature*.

TETRALOGY. See *trilogy*.

THEOLOGY. See *myth*.

THINK PIECE. A thematic story, as distinguished from a piece of *journalism* with the same designation that relies on exposition, analysis, and editorial opinion.

THRILLER. See *action fiction*.

TRANSCRIPTION. See *adaptation*.

TRILOGY. A series of three novels; a tetralogy is a series of four.

TRIPLE-DECKER. Also called a double-decker, this type of novel is a book of exceedingly great length, like those written by such modern authors as James Michener and Danielle Steel or those that were written as serials in the nineteenth century by William Makepeace Thackeray and Charles Dickens.

TRUE HISTORIES. During the seventeenth and early eighteenth centuries the idea of serious fiction was not yet completely acceptable socially; therefore, many novels were published as "*true histories*." Those that were not appeared as "romances," often with prefaces that argued for their legitimacy by referring to Aristotle's principles. The "true histories" purported to be what they were not; they were, in fact, pseudo-autobiographies detailing the adventures of a real person, as in Daniel Defoe's *Moll Flanders* (1660–1731).

UTOPIAN NOVEL. A form invented by the sixteenth-century English martyr Thomas More (1478–1535) that posits an "ideal" society for hortatory or satirical purposes and may be considered an early form of *science fiction*. Its prototype was *The Republic* of Plato (427?–347? B.C.). Modern examples are *Looking

Backward by Edward Bellamy (1850–1898) and *1984* by George Orwell (1903–1950), although the neologism dystopia has been coined to distinguish between an "ideal" society and an evil version of such a community; the term would be applied to Orwell's novel and to William Golding's *Lord of the Flies*.

VERISIMILITUDE. A *style* used by both Realists and Naturalists, the term means "to give the IMPRESSION of real life," the emphasis being on "impression."

VIGNETTE. A finely written literary sketch emphasizing character, situation, or scene.

WELL-BUILT STORY. In recent years called also the workshop story, it is one that observes the formula that all four of the elements of fiction—plot, theme, atmosphere, and character—will be present and supportive of one another.

WESTERNS. Novels or stories set in the western regions of the United States, particularly during the late nineteenth century and the great era of the cowboys and the Indians, the ranchers and the sheepherders, the gunfighters and the outlaws, and the sheriffs and rangers who attempted to keep peace among them.

WORKSHOP STORY. See *well-built story*.

YARN. See *tall tale*.

The Genres of Drama

There are several subgenres of the literary genre called drama. The first type of drama in the Western world apparently grew out of ceremonial music as it was performed in sixth-century-B.C. Greece, in the region of Athens; thus, the first "plays" were *musical theater*. The Greek poet Thespis invented a form of music that required a character, which he himself portrayed, and a chorus; these interacted with one another, telling a tragic story by means of dialogue, song, and dance. This form of drama was soon so popular that in 534 B.C. a theatrical competition was held, in honor of Dionysus, the god of drink, fertility, and revelry, to decide the best new tragedy written by the playwrights of the period. Such contests soon became annual events throughout the Greek world, including perhăps Hellenic Egypt, for it has been postulated that the Book of Job of the Old Testament was originally a Greek tragedy, and it has been so reconstructed in the twentieth century.

Over five hundred tragedies were written in ancient Greece, but only thirty-two have survived. Aeschylus added a second character to the *cast* of the Thespian play in the fifth century B.C., and Sophocles added a third. These innovations allowed the *playwright* to compose works that were infinitely more complex psychologically and more active dramatically. Clearly, the form of tragedy was continually evolving, but in the fourth century B.C.

Aristotle, in his *Poetics,* analyzed the work of Sophocles as typical tragedies, in effect freezing the form, as it were, for the study of scholars and tragedians. Nevertheless, tragedy continued to develop in the works of Hippolytus, Euripides, and others; and other types of plays were added to the programs of the ancient competitions, including burlesques such as the *satyr play,* which was ribald, satirical, and slapstick and was performed after every third tragedy just to provide some relief for the tensions that had been building up in the audience throughout the performances.

Eventually, there were other types of plays being performed as well, such as *comedies,* the first of which we call *old comedy* and examples of which were written by Aristophanes in the fifth century B.C. This type of theatrical piece was succeeded by the *new comedy* of Menander. In the original tragedies and in the satyr plays and old comedies, the characters had been either idealizations, lampoons, or caricatures of people; but Menander injected an element of *realism* into his productions, and his *personae* became recognizable as actual people involved in complex situations and actions. The importance of the chorus and many other elements of the early drama diminished. All the elements still associated not only with drama but with fiction as well were present in the new comedy.

The fiction writer and the *playwright* have much in common. Both are concerned with *narrative,* and both use exactly the same elements of narrative: *character, plot, atmosphere,* and *theme.* However, unlike fiction, drama is a composite genre, consisting of both written material and visual effects. The strengths of drama enable it to be more immediately apprehensible to the senses than are words in a book.

The fiction writer is not limited to one or two *writing techniques* but may choose from a wide range of narrative devices. The dramatist's range of writing techniques, however, is limited, for all that may be used onstage is spoken language, not ordinary *narration* or *description,* except as spoken by an actor or actress; though on occasion a play—such as *Our Town* by Thornton Wilder—may have a *narrator* on the stage filling in the *exposition*: background information that the audience may need in order to understand the significance of the dramatic segments. The writing tools of the playwright, then, are *dialogue, monologue, soliloquy* and the *aside*.

In place of narration, however, the playwright is able to utilize *stage action,* and in place of description the dramatist provides *acts, scenes,* and *sets* so that the *audience* can actually see and hear the development of character and plot. At this point in our discussion a consideration of Greek tragedy as it was analyzed by Aristotle may be of some value, for it is the paradigm on which all later drama was founded.

Tragedy

The major and original *subgenre* of *dramatic literature* is *tragedy*, a dramatic form out of classical antiquity, the elements of which are *plot, character, spectacle, thought, diction,* and *harmony* (i.e., the successful *fusion* of its parts). Tragedy, according to Aristotle, is the *imitation* of a "worthy or illustrious and perfect *action.*" It has "*magnitude*" and is written in *elevated language* that *entertains,* but it is not meant to be read, for it must be *enacted* on the stage. It is a *verse drama,* which has as its *protagonist* (generally but not always male) the *tragic hero* or *heroine,* who has stature but does not excel in either virtue or justice; nor is he or she brought low through such character flaws as vice or depravity but through some error of judgment or circumstance, at which point a sudden reversal, a *peripety,* occurs. The *heroic protagonist* struggles to avoid inevitable defeat (*fate*), and during the struggle *sympathy* and *terror* are held in *equilibrium* as he (or sometimes she) courageously faces *the human predicament.* Tragedy exhibits the *paradox* of nobility of character combined with human fallibility, especially *hubris*—excessive pride or self-confidence, a *tragic flaw.*

Ostensibly, the *antagonist* of tragedy is a god, or the gods, but in fact the antagonist is *destiny,* which is in the hands of the three *fates: Clotho,* who bears the distaff that holds the threads of life, *Lachesis,* who spins the thread, and *Atropos,* who cuts the thread when the time comes to do so. This destiny is often bound up with past actions on the part of the protagonist, as in Sophocles' *Oedipus Rex*, in which case the struggle of the play becomes an *internal struggle*, so the overt conflict is interior: Oedipus is locked in mortal combat with himself, with his past, and with the past actions of his ancestors, which he has inherited.

Although the protagonist is heroic and as such is in a way godlike, he or she is also human, and human beings are fallible. Achilles, who is the hero of Homer's *Iliad* (an epic, not a tragedy), was the offspring of Peleus and the minor goddess Thetis, who dipped Achilles in the river Styx so that, like the gods, he would be invulnerable. But the heel by which Thetis held him when she dipped him in the magic river that forms the boundary of Hades, the *netherworld*, was not touched by the water, and he therefore remained humanly vulnerable, and mortal, in just this one part of his anatomy. It was in this heel that he was eventually fatally wounded by Paris. Thus, most heroic protagonists have a flaw, and that flaw, symbolized by the heel of Achilles, leads to *doom*. The *tragic flaw* is usually not physical, however; it may be pride, a lapse in judgment, arrogance, or some other *moral flaw*, and the protagonist may not even be aware that it exists.

Aristotle believed that the opposite of pity is *nemesan*, or "righteous indignation," but logically the opposite of pity is *envy*. In any case, whatever the flaw, it not only leads to doom, but it is also the instrument by which *Nemesis*, the goddess of retributive justice, eventually expunges disorder in the universe. Things must be set right—morally right. Sin cannot be allowed to exist in human affairs forever. Good must eventually win, evil lose. Generally speaking, the protagonist must resolve his or her own dilemmas as the incidents of the play are worked out, but on occasion both the Greek and Roman playwrights called into use the *deus ex machina*, which was a god who was lowered by stage machinery out of the heavens onto the stage to help the hero or heroine out of a difficult situation. (Such devices would operate to destroy the *willing suspension of disbelief* of the contemporary playgoer.)

Since the *heroic protagonist* of tragedy is essentially good but is also the bearer of evil, he or she must be punished; it is this paradox that gives tragedy its *dramatic tension*. The audience will see the *fall from grace* of a great figure, and the fall will be mighty. It will be an anguished fall; the *audience* is meant to sense the irony of the situation, the passion of such a moral spectacle. The hero or heroine recognizes the fact of impending doom, often in the shape of a person who bears the message of the protagonist's fate. Perhaps the protagonist will attempt to rectify what is clearly coming, but that attempt produces the opposite effect, hastening doom instead; this is called *peripeteia*. Once the *climax* of the drama has occurred—that is, the final *rising action* in a series of rising actions—and the fall has taken place, the universe will have again been set right, and the audience should sense the essential rightness of the protagonist's destruction. Despite the feeling that a *mortal injustice* has taken place, a higher, or *poetic, justice* has been served, and this sense of cosmic justice leads to a *purging* of the emotions of fear and pity that have been called into play by the actions of the drama and the character of the protagonist. In the *denouement* of the play the loose ends of the plot will be drawn together and the tragedy brought to a close.

Structure

The parts of a tragedy are the *prologue*, *parados*, *episode*, *exode*, and *chorus*. The prologue is all of the first portion of a tragedy that precedes the entrance of the chorus, which is the parados (*parade*). An episode is that portion of the tragedy that takes place between two complete *choral odes*. The exode (*exodos*) is that portion of a tragedy that follows the last song of the chorus.

The *stasimon* is the song sung by the chorus as it enters from the side of the stage; the *parados* is the first speech of the complete chorus, not counting speeches by members of the chorus. The *choral ode* itself is constructed of three parts, the first of which is the *strophe*. The second movement, called the *antistrophe*, is identical in *structure* to the first. The third and last movement of the poem is called the *stand,* or *epode*. Its form is strict, like the first two movements, but entirely different from them in structure.

The content of the strophe is an argument in favor of a *viewpoint,* which is spoken by a chorus on one side of the stage. To consider the opposite view, the chorus travels to the other side of the stage to deliver the antistrophe, through which it voices its concerns; or there is a second chorus on the opposite side of the stage that does the same. In the epode the chorus moves to center stage to deliver its conclusion on the matter under consideration.

The Unities

Greek drama sometimes observed the *unities* of *action, place,* and *time,* though later plays seldom did so. The *unity of action* concerns the plot, which must have a *beginning,* a *middle,* and an *end,* and it must be of a proper proportion, neither too long, nor too short: long enough to amply treat the *theme* of the play but not long enough to bore the audience. The plot must be a *unified series of actions,* beginning with the *protasis,* in which the major characters are introduced and the subject delineated. The drama begins *in medias res* (in the middle of the *inciting action,* background information or *exposition* being offered as the play progresses), all of which lead to the protagonist's *doom,* which is not a matter of *suspense,* for the audience already knows the protagonist will be destroyed, for it is a matter of history or mythology. It is the spectacle of his or her downfall that enthralls the *spectators.*

The *unity of time* is a *convention,* a social agreement; it assumes that, during the *theatrical time* of the play, one day—no more than twenty-four hours—will have elapsed. If the play asks the audience to believe that larger segments of time pass while the audience is seated in the theater watching, their *willing suspension of disbelief,* the *dramatic illusion,* will be imperiled.

The *unity of place* is a convention that all action will take place in one location and setting, for the audience's willing suspension of disbelief and the Greek theatre's lack of elaborate stage equipment required that there be a minimum of shifting from scene to scene, although the *skene* allowed the representation of scenes in an inner chamber or cave. The various areas around the stage could be used to suggest a variety of exterior settings.

Comedy

Comedy, which also dates from the *Classical period*, is tragedy *lampooned*, as in the *satyr play* (see *satire*), which, in classical Greek theater, was a *mock-tragedy* that followed the performance of three tragedies. The *dramatis personae* of a satyr play were satyrs: half-men, half-goats, with the tails of horses. The protagonist of any comedy is a humorous, not an empathetic, character, and the stages by which he or she progresses toward defeat or possibly triumph are humorous as well.

There are two kinds of classical comedy extant: *old comedy* and *new comedy*; examples of *middle comedy*, which apparently was transitional between the two, did not survive into the modern world. An example of old comedy is Aristophanes' *The Birds,* which combines *satire, ribaldry, fantasy, parody (caricature, pastiche,* or *lampoon*), and *travesty (burlesque).* The *aside*, a device of old comedy, allowed the chorus to address the audience directly and to speak from the viewpoint of the author. Menander's new comedy, which has survived only in fragments, has a comic plot in which, generally, young lovers work out the problems that divide them and come together at last.

The division of modern dramas into *acts* and *scenes* may have been foreshadowed by the division of the *classical tragedy* into *episodes* separated by *choral odes. Dramatic action* is generally considered to proceed in five parts, *exposition, complication, climax, falling action (denouement),* and *catastrophe,* and it may be for this reason that Roman drama consisted of five acts, one correponding to each of these parts. Freytag's *pyramid* (see figure) is a diagram of the five-act drama.

Classical drama continued in the work of the Roman playwrights, which succeeded and imitated the Greek tragedians and comedians; but the religious element of the Greek plays, which had been diminishing anyway as time went by, was further eroded in the work of the first important Roman dramatist, Livius Andronicus, in the third century B.C. His plays were clearly intended

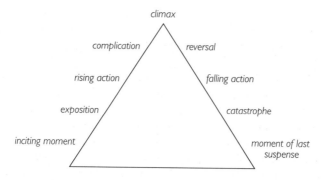

primarily as entertainment, as were those of Plautus, who was not so much an original author as an adaptor of the plays of the Greek new comedy. In many of the Roman plays other elements were added, often including florid speech, spectacular stage effects, farce, stock characters, and mime. Many of these additions were derived from southern Italian and Sicilian Greek commercial pantomime theater, which was obscene and ludicrous. However, there was also a serious tradition in Roman drama, which was exemplified in the second century B.C. by the work of Terence and, in the first centuries B.C./A.D., by that of Seneca.

Eventually, Roman theater died with its empire, and the Middle Ages ensued, with completely different forms of drama that returned to its original religious roots. *Liturgical drama* (q.v.) included *miracle plays, morality plays, mystery plays*—performed in *cycles*, such as the English Wakefield Cycle—and *passion plays*. Secular *folk plays* also were written and performed during the medieval period.

During the succeeding Renaissance, comedy and tragedy were rediscovered and rehabilitated, and all sorts of conglomerates were invented. These included *academic drama* or *school plays* and *revenge tragedies; histories* or *chronicle plays, comedies of errors,* and *tragicomedies,* like those written by William Shakespeare; and *masques,* the great English master of which was Ben Jonson.

The English theater was killed during the Commonwealth period, but the English Restoration brought with it the *heroic drama;*

the ensuing drama included the last plays of the tradition of the Italian *burletta*, the *comedy of manners*, and the new *critical comedy*, as well as a revival of the classical tragedy (e.g., *Irene,* written by Samuel Johnson).

The five-act drama invented by the Roman playwrights lasted until the late nineteenth century, when the Norwegian playwright Henrik Ibsen invented the *thesis drama* or *problem play* and changed form by combining the fourth and fifth acts. The *romantic tragedy* is a phenomenon of the twentieth century, as is the three-act drama; *musical comedy* and *comic opera* are often written in two acts. The one-act play is also a twentieth-century phenomenon. All these types of plays and others are discussed briefly in the Chapter Glossary.

Dialogue

The primary means by which drama proceeds is *dialogue*, which is conversation among the characters of the play. Dialogue in ancient Greek tragedy and poetry is sometimes arranged as *stichomythia*, the alternation of lines spoken by actors. A *monologue* is half of a *conversation*, a *speech* to a character who is presumed to be present, though a listener may not be evident to the audience (e.g., if the *actor* or *actress* on the stage is speaking into a telephone). A *monodrama* is, first, a *dramatic monologue*; second, a sequence of dramatic monologues by various characters who relate a story, as in the stage version of Edgar Lee Masters's *Spoon River*; and, third, a *one-man show* or theatrical presentation featuring only one actor. If the playwright wishes to convey directly to the audience an interior state—thoughts or emotions—he or she must use the *soliloquy* or the *aside,* a remark directed toward the audience in a *stage whisper* loud enough for the audience to hear but, supposedly, not the other personae on stage. A *soliloquy,* sometimes called an *interior monologue*, is differentiated from a dramatic monologue in that it is personal thoughts verbalized rather than half a conversation; it is "talking to oneself," for no other audience is present or assumed to be present. However, those thoughts or feelings may be objectified in actions; for instance, if a character thinks she is ugly, after looking into a mirror she may break it angrily.

Dialogue is indicated by means of a *script,* which contains not only all of the dialogue of the play but the *actions* and *stage directions* as well and indications of the *acts, scenes, sets,* and *settings,* placement and kind of *props, stage business,* and so forth. An *antiplay* is one that violates all the rules of drama, like those written for the *theater of the absurd,* which is a *mirror image* of a traditional play.

In his trend-setting *Six Characters in Search of an Author,* the *playwright* Luigi Pirandello has one of his *personae,* The Father, say at one point, "Oh, Sir, you know well that life is full of infinite absurdities, which, strangely enough, do not even need to appear plausible, since they are true." This speech puts into a capsule the philosophy of *existentialism,* which is at the basis of much *Modernist* literature, including the so-called *theater of the absurd* and *black humor.* All but one of the things that are a part of the *traditional theater* are called into question. *Traditional drama* assumes, like all *traditional literature,* that there is a *cause-and-effect* relationship among the *incidents* of a *plot* and that this relationship gives the *audience* an accurate reflection of reality, what Aristotle called *mimesis (imitatio)* and what in the nineteenth century was called *Realism.* Thus, a character in *fiction* or *drama* has a *dominant personality trait,* a *desire,* or *motivation,* a *problem* to solve, and his or her attempts at a solution of the problem provide the *dramatic situation,* the *conflict* and the *plot* of the *narrative.* What happens, however, if our experience causes us to sympathize with the view of Pirandello's "Father"? Then one need not act rationally; in fact, it would be strange if one did so in most situations. Life is full of gratuitous occurrences—there is no obvious *beginning* or *end* of any *series of actions.*

There are, indeed, such things as *accidents* and *coincidences,* both of which are banned from "realistic" literature on the grounds that the audience will not believe they can have occurred if they affect the outcome of the story, for the story, in order to be convincing, must be *truer to life than life,* and the *protagonist* must solve his or her own problem without resorting to a *deus ex machina* to help in a difficult situation. If, however, writers fail to show such things in their narratives, they are not, in fact, being simply "true to life." By excluding the absurdity of real life, writers are not giving an accurate picture of life at all. It's all *illusion*, *artifice*. The theater of the absurd puts its finger on the basic premise of traditional art and says, "This won't do. If life is absurd and art is rational, the one cannot mirror the other."

Much theater of the absurd says, therefore, "Let there be no *characterizations*, no *plot*, no *atmosphere*; let there be no *motivation*, for desires are irrational at root. Let the impossible happen, without reason, for that is what happens in life as often as not. Let there be no *exposition*, for what has happened in the past does not necessarily have a bearing on the present situation; and even if it does, most of it is accident and happenstance anyway."

At this point one might ask oneself, "But is such literature *art*?" And the answer is "No." Then what is it? Perhaps one can answer the question by replying, "It is *anti-art*," which is to say, it is art after all.

That may seem paradoxical, and it is, but a *paradox* is a self-contradictory statement that is nevertheless true, and literature of the absurd is paradox, just as life is. Anti-art is nothing but the *mirror image* of art, **but it could not exist without something to reflect**. If one takes all the conventions of traditional art and reverses them, one is still reflecting a *pattern*, and the mirror image will be a pattern also—a pattern in reverse.

There is one element of traditional art, however, that no one seems to be able to dispense with, and that is *theme*. Pirandello's play is, in many ways, not merely a an excellent play out of theater of the absurd but an essay on the art of the absurd as well. It is *metadrama*: a play that is also a treatise in paradox. It is an attack on traditional literature, and the very situation of the play sets the paradox: six characters out of an unwritten play break up the performance of a drama, and they ask the actors to produce *their* drama, a *play within a play*, and they want someone, the *director* (or *manager*) to write their story. They insist on "truth," and it becomes clear that drama is incapable of presenting the truth as it appears to the characters. In fact, the truth appears to be different not only to the actors and the manager, but to each individual character as well. Art is thus a compromise, and the play asks the question "Can a compromise be true to life?" The query is a *rhetorical question*, one to which the answer is known by all who hear it.

CHAPTER GLOSSARY

Italicized terms are glossed elsewhere in the book; see index.

ACADEMIC DRAMA. Classical and original dramas produced in the colleges and grammar schools of England during the Renaissance, also called school plays. Two of the earliest known original school plays are the anonymous *Gammer Gurton's Needle* (ca. 1560) and *Ralph Roister Doister* by Nicholas Udall (1505–56).

ACT. A major division of a play, which may consist of more than one *scene*. See *screenplay* and *teleplay*. See also discussion of drama in text.

ACTION. Movement, doing things, deeds. For the various ramifications of the word, see *camera techniques*, *epitasis*, *point of attack*, and *praxis*.

ACTOR, ACTRESS. Persons who perform roles in a play. See *dramatis personae*.

ADAPTATION. The product of one who turns one form of literature into another, for instance, a novel into a cinema production.

ADAPTOR. One who performs adaptation. See *backstage*.

AGON. The classical Greek term for struggle. See *conflict*, *dramatic situation*, and *opposition*.

AGROIKOS. See *dramatis personae*.

ALAZON. See *dramatis personae*.

AMATEUR PLAYER. One who acts in plays but is not a professional actor. See *masque*.

AMATEUR SHOOTING. See *camera techniques*.

AMPHITHEATER. An outdoor *theater*.

ANAGNORISIS. The classical Greek term for the protagonist of a tragedy's recognition of his or her impending doom.

ANGEL. A wealthy person who, for one reason or another, invests in theatrical or cinematic productions.

ANTAGONIST. That which opposes the protagonist. See *dramatic situation* and *dramatis personae*.

ANTIMASQUE. The opposite of a *masque*.

APRON. The lip of the stage forward of the *curtain,* which marks the *proscenium arch* proper.

ARENA THEATER. Theater-in-the-round. See *theater.*

ARIA. A song in a musical production, in particular an *opera.*

ASIDE. A remark or comment made directly to the audience by an actor, by convention assumed not to have been heard by the cast onstage.

AUDITORIUM. A combination stage and lecture hall; see *theater.*

AUTEUR. A *director* who, like Alfred Hitchcock, imposes his personal stamp and vision on a film (*auteur* is French for "author"), demoting the screenwriter, the author of the filmscript, to second rank creatively. See also *camera techniques.*

BACKCLOTH, BACKDROP. A painted scenic curtain hung at the rear of the stage. See *scene* and *stage.*

BACKLIGHT. Lighting from the rear of the stage. See *lighting.*

BACKSTAGE. Behind the scenes. The backstage crew are the people who are involved in *mounting* a play on the stage. "Backstage" also denotes an area of the theater behind the *stage* proper.

BALANCE. Equilibrium, offsetting tensions. See *stasis.*

BALCONY. The tier of seats above the main floor of a *theater.*

BALLAD OPERA. A type of *light opera.*

BIG SCREEN. *Cinema,* as distinguished from the small screen, *television.*

BITS. Routines in comedies.

BLACK COMEDY. A twentieth century phenomenon, it is the theatrical equivalent of black humor in fiction. Theater of the absurd is typically black comedy; see the discussion of Luigi Pirandello's *Six Characters in Search of an Author,* which is also an example of *metadrama.*

BLACK MOMENT. That point in a *screenplay* when the chances of the protagonist hang in the balance.

BLACKFACE. Makeup used in a *minstrel show*.

BLACKOUT. A technique of *film editing* by means of which the screen goes momentarily black. There may also be a stage blackout.

BLOCKING. The disposition of the players and their movements, scene by scene. See *director* and *mise-en-scène*.

BLOCKING CHARACTER. A secondary *antagonist*. See *dramatis personae*.

BOMB. To fail badly; a failed dramatic production.

BOMOLOCHOS. See *dramatis personae*.

BON MOT. A witty bit of repartee such as is to be found in *high comedy*.

BOURGEOIS DRAMA. A synonym for *melodrama*.

BOX, BOXES. Private seating in a *theater*.

BOX OFFICE. The spot in a *theater* where tickets are sold.

BOX SET. A particular arrangement for a play's *set*.

BOYISH HERO. The protagonist of a *melodrama*.

BROADWAY MUSICAL. The American version of a *musical*.

BROADWAY THEATER. The *theater* in which the most prestigious American plays are performed. Broadway theater is the goal of every American playwright, as the *theatre district* is for British dramatists.

BURLESQUE SHOW, BURLEY-CUE. The burlesque show, sometimes called the "burley-cue" by its *vaudeville* patrons, contained songs, skits, dances, satire of current events, and comic acts. It was a vulgar version of the *revue*. See *musical comedy* and *revue*.

BURLETTA. Also called *ballad opera*, a form of *musical comedy* containing broad humor, rhyming dialogue, and new lyrics set to old tunes. It survived until the eighteenth century in the work of such playwrights as John Gay (1685–1732) whose *The Beggar's Opera* was revived in the twentieth century as Kurt Weill's *Dreigroschenoper* (*Threepenny Opera*).

BUSKINS. One of two items of costume that have become synonyms for tragedy and comedy: buskins were "lift-boots" worn by tragic actors to give them more height, and *socks* were worn by comic actors to decrease their size.

CAMEO. A small role played by a famous actor or other celebrity.

CAMEO ACTOR. A famous player, usually in motion pictures, who appears briefly; for instance, Alfred Hitchcock, the motion picture director who always gave himself a cameo role in his movies.

CAMERA ANGLES. The *long shot* is a panoramic camera angle focusing on an action or object at a distance, sometimes called the establishing shot because it sets up the scene and situation. To pan the camera is to move it to follow the action at a distance. The *medium shot* shows the object in context from a closer angle, for instance, lovers kissing in a sylvan bower. The *close-up* is a shot that gets very near its focused object. If the object is seen from above or below, the camera is taking a *tilt shot* up or down. A *high-angle shot* is a tilt-down shot, and a *low-angle shot* is a tilt-up shot, both from a considerable distance. The *zoom shot* races in from a distance, the *tracking* or *traveling shot* follows a moving object, sometimes from a crane (a crane shot). A *freeze* is the movie equivalent of a photographic still shot, that is to say, it is a snapshot or a portrait embedded in a moving picture ("still shots" are used to publicize movies in theater lobbies and elsewhere). A *soft focus* means a deliberately blurry camera focus, either of the whole shot or of the background or foreground of the shot, for particular purposes, such as not to show an actress's poor complexion in a close-up.

CAMERA TECHNIQUES. A *shot* is that part of a television or film production that corresponds with a scene in a stage play, or that represents one complete camera *roll* between the director's call for *action* and his order to *cut*. Normal *film projection speed* is twenty-four frames per second; if it is projected at anything less, it is being shown in *slow motion (slomo)*.

CAST. The *dramatis personae* of a play.

CATASTASIS. The classical Greek term for *climax*.

CATASTROPHE. The classical Greek term for the winding-up, or *denouement,* of the plot of a tragedy.

CATHARSIS. The classical Greek term for a purgation of the emotions of the viewers of a tragedy.

CHAMBER OPERA. A one-act opera requiring a minimum of characters, scenes, and musicians.

CHARACTER ACTOR. One of the *dramatis personae* who portrays a particular type of person, other than the protagonist or antagonist of a play.

CHORAGOS. The leader of the *chorus*. See also *dramatis personae*.

CHOREOGRAPHED MOVEMENT. Dance. See *masque* and *noh play*.

CHORUS. Led by the *choragos*, the chorus is the *vox populi*, the voice of the people, discussing the situation of the tragic hero. Aristotle said that it is necessary to consider the chorus as one of the characters of the tragedy, for as a whole it interacts with the *protagonist* and the other dramatis personae, complementing them and extending the drama. See *tragedy* in the chapter text, and *opera*.

CHRONICLE PLAY. Also *history play,* a late Elizabethan historical drama based on Holinshed's *Chronicles* and other books of the period having to do with events of British history. Such stage productions were full of spectacle, pageant (flamboyant display), and scenes of warfare. They were didactic in nature and took as their subject matter historical situations arranged in chronological order. Though chronicle plays often dealt with people of high rank, they were neither tragedy nor comedy, and they were aimed at a popular, not an aristocratic, audience.

CINEMA. Motion pictures, moving pictures, the movies, "the silver screen."

CINEMA VERITÉ. *Direct cinema,* utilizing camera techniques and materials such as *fast film* (which is grainier than *slow film*) that simulate amateur shooting and film developing so as to give the audience the impression that the scenes depicted were caught by passersby through happenstance. The idea is to lead the viewer to believe that there is a certain element of sincerity in what is being seen in a cinema or television production.

CLIFFHANGER. A *melodrama* that depends on suspense.

CLIMAX. The ultimate conflict between the *protagonist,* or hero, of a drama, and the *antagonist,* or opponent, of the protagonist. See *screenplay*.

CLOSED ENDING. A neatly tied-up conclusion to a play. See *intrusion*.

CLOSET DRAMA. A play written particularly to be read rather than produced. See *problem play*.

CLOSE-UP. A near *camera angle*.

COLLOQUY. A synonym for *dialogue*.

COMEDY. Many comic plays are examples of *low comedy*, as is the Italian seventeenth-century *commedia dell'arte,* which was a form of *improvisational theater* that depended on a scenario that specified entrances and exits but otherwise allowed the actors to draw on stock *dramatis personae* such as Pantalone the merchant; a pair of servants, one (Arlecchino) clever, and one (Pulcinella) foolish; the physician, Graziano; and of course, young lovers. This sort of theater also relied on *bits* (stock situations and lines) and pieces of *stage business* called *lazzi* (in the plural; *lazzo* in the singular).

COMEDY OF ERRORS. A play that postulates a complex plot that depends heavily on coincidence—serendipitous occurrences—but that eventually works out to the happy ending wherein the knots are unraveled and the lovers are united.

COMEDY OF HUMOURS. The humours were the ancient bodily secretions believed to control the personalities of people: blood, phlegm, black bile, and yellow bile. The *comedy of humours* had stock characters that represented types of people (stereotypes) whose humors were out of balance, such as the *miles gloriosus,* or swaggering warrior; the *senex iratus,* or angry father; the *dolosus servus,* or crafty servant; the greedy miser; the foolish spendthrift; the jealous husband, and so forth.

COMEDY OF MANNERS. A type of *high comedy* that mocks the behavior of the upper classes.

COMEDY OF MORALS. A type of *critical comedy* that skewers hypocrisy.

COMEDY OF WIT. A type of *high comedy* that relies primarily on clever dialogue rather than on action.

COMIC OPERA. A synonym for *light opera*.

COMIC RELIEF. Intervals of comedy or humor in tragedies, said to provide a lessening of tension but often, in fact, by contrast increasing the tension or the terror of the drama.

COMIC SCRIPT. A screenplay for a *sitcom* or other *teleplay* or cinema comedy.

COMMEDIA DELL'ARTE. Comedies in the comic tradition of Italian theater.

COMMERCIAL MESSAGE. A television advertisement. See *teleplay*.

COMPLICATION. An element that entangles the plot of a play, in particular a *tragicomedy*.

COMPOUND MODE. The use of more than one type of performance in a drama—for instance, dialogue, song, dance, and mime, as in the *masque* and *noh play*, or a combination of prose and verse in the script.

CONFLICT. The *agon,* or contest occurring between the protagonist and antagonist of a drama, resulting in a dramatic situation.

COSMIC IRONY. Intervention by the gods or fate, providing the solution to a problem a moment too late or at an inappropriate moment, as when, in a comedy, the *deus ex machina* descends to rescue the protagonist who is just taking his last breath.

COSTUME, COSTUMIER. The costumier designs and supervises the making of costumes.

COUNTERPLAYER. A member of the *dramatis personae* of a play who plots against the protagonist.

COUP DE THÉÂTRE. A stunning reversal of fortune in *heroic drama.* The actors who filled these *roles* would *emote* (overact) and *upstage* (overshadow) one another, delivering their lines with *bombast* (inflated oratorical style).

COURT COMEDY. A relative of the *masque,* written to be played at the court of Elizabeth I.

CRANE SHOT. See *camera angles.*

CRISIS. A rising action of a play or *screenplay.*

CRITICAL COMEDY. Satires like Molière's *Tartuffe,* which attacks religious hypocrisy, sometimes called *comedies of morals.*

CROWD SCENE. In a cinema or television production, a shot of an assemblage of people of some sort involving those *dramatis personae* called extras.

CURTAIN. The device that separates the audience from the *stage.*

CURTAIN RAISER. Any preliminary presentation or short play preceding the beginning of the *main feature.*

CUT. A fast-transition *camera technique* in *film editing.*

CUTAWAY. A feature of the box *set*.

DENOUEMENT. The result of a series of events or episodes in a drama, the resolution of the plot.

DEUS EX MACHINA. A *stage device* that allows the gods to descend out of the heavens into the midst of a play.

DEUTERAGONIST. A secondary character in a tragedy. See *dramatis personae*.

DIALOGUE. Spoken conversation among characters in a play.

DIANOIA. The classical Greek term for *thought*.

DINNER THEATER. A type of twentieth-century theater-cum-restaurant where both plays and food are served.

DIRECT CINEMA. A synonym for *cinema verité*. See *camera techniques*.

DIRECTOR. One who oversees the artistic aspects of a drama or movie and supervises its production, including its blocking; see also *auteur*.

DISGUISINGS. *Masques* performed in the schools (see *academic drama*).

DISQUISITORY DRAMA. A synonym for *problem play*.

DISSOLVE. A type of *film editing* in which one scene slowly disappears from the screen as another grows to take its place.

DIVERTISSEMENT. An *entr'acte* to distract the audience while the scene is changed or while an intermission is in progress.

DOCUDRAMA. A cross between a *documentary*, the depiction of actual events, and a fictive play based on such events.

DOCUMENTARY. A film or television program based on facts and presented in an informative manner. It may consist of *interviews* and news clips presented by a narrator.

DOLOSUS SERVUS. A member of the cast of a *comedy of humours*.

DOMESTIC TRAGEDY. A synonym for *romantic tragedy*.

DOWNSTAGE. The area closest to the audience, near the *pit*, where the musicians are situated beneath the stage.

DRAMATIC SCRIPT. A *teleplay*.

DRAMATIC SITUATION. The desire, on the part of a *protagonist*, to be, to have, or to do something, together with the *opposition* of an *antagonist*—another person, a circumstance, or a condition, resulting in an *agon* or *conflict* that must reach a resolution. See the chapter "The Genres of Fiction" for a more complete discussion of this term.

DRAMATIS PERSONAE. The characters of the drama played by *actors* and *actresses*, the *cast* of the play, including the *leading man* and *leading lady*, *character actors* and actresses, and other members, such as *counterplayers* who plot against the protagonist. The personae of tragedy have been discussed above; they are masked or *stylized characters* who are representatives not of abstractions as such but, first, of historical or mythological figures and, second, of types of people (see *typecasting*), plus one or sometimes two *choruses*, usually representative of the citizens, that comment on the action.

Types of characters to be found in Greek literature other than the protagonist and the antagonist are the *agroikos,* or dour rustic; the *alazon,* or braggart; the *bomolochos,* or clown; the *deuteragonist* and *tritagonist,* or second and third most important personae of the drama; the *eiron,* or dissembling confidant; and the *senex* or *senex iratus*, a *blocking character* other than the antagonist who tends to stand in the way of the the protagonist's achieving his or her desire.

DRAMATURGE. The *translator* of a play or its adaptor from another medium or language. May also simply be a synonym for playwright.

DRAME. Another word to describe a *problem play*.

DRAWING ROOM COMEDY. A *high comedy* whose humor derives from the antics of the uppercrust.

DUBBING. A term that may mean various things: the superaddition of music, sound effects, or voice to a film; the substitution of voice *dialogue* in a different language from the original language used in a film; or even a voice-over. In cinema and television we are used to watching characters in action and hearing a voice dubbed in over the action that lets us hear what is in the character's mind while he or she is doing whatever is being done. Actually, the voice-over is an adaptation of narrative technique and can be used in stage drama as well.

DUET. An *opera* highlight sung by two people.

DUMB SHOW. An interlude of *pantomime* within a spoken drama. See also *masque* and *noh play*.

EIRON. A member of the *dramatis personae* of a play who is the dissembling confidante of the protagonist.

EMOTING. Overacting, as in a *melodrama*.

ENDING. The conclusion of a play, which may be either closed, with all loose ends tied up, or open, that is, ending ambiguously. The latter sorts of endings are generally to be found in the modern period. See *intrusion*.

ENSEMBLE. Musicians, singers, dancers, or actors performing in a group. See *opera*.

ENTR'ACTE. The period of time separating the acts of a play; also a *divertissement*—a ballet or other *interlude,* such as a *plampede*, a *harlequinade* (a clown drama), or a *pantomime*, which are short plays, generally satiric or comic in nature, performed between the acts of a longer play, often a tragedy.

EPISODE. One scene or action in a related series, for instance, one incident in a plot. See *melodrama*.

EPITASIS. The classical Greek term for *rising action*.

ESTABLISHING SHOT. See *camera angles*.

EXTRA. The least members of the cast of a motion picture are the extras who are used to fill out a *crowd scene*.

EXTRAVAGANZA. An entertainment or performance that relies on spectacle, music, and elaborate display. See *musical*.

F/X. *Special effects* in cinema and television.

FADE, FADE-IN, FADE-OUT. A gradual lightening or dimming of the scene in cinema and television. See *film editing*.

FARCE. Light, broad comedy that depends on a fast-paced and intricate plot, stereotyped characters, even *slapstick*—collisions, chases, *pratfalls,* and physical assault, as in the puppet plays called *Punch and Judy shows,* in which the puppets slap each other with paddles (the origin of the term, "slapstick").

FAST FILM. A type of film that does not require much light. See *film speed*.

FATE WORSE THAN DEATH. What may happen to the heroine if she is caught in the clutches of the villain of the piece. See *melodrama.*

FEATURE TELEVISION SCRIPT. A major *teleplay.*

FILM EDITING. *Cuts* are transitions within a film between scenes or shots. A *straight cut* is the immediate transition from one scene or shot to another, with nothing intervening, corresponding to a *blackout* in the theater, which is more rapid than the "lights down and out" direction. In the *dissolve* one scene fades into the succeeding scene, whereas in the *fade* (*fade-in* or *-out*) the *screen* (the television screen or the "big screen") wanes to black before the next scene waxes to full. With the rapid expansion of special effects, all sorts of fades, dissolves, blackouts, and more innovative transitions are possible, including old effects like the *wipe*, in which one scene takes over the screen from the left or right as the old scene is wiped off it; the *iris;* which appears as a central insert on the screen and expands until it has forced the last scene out of the edges of the picture. A virtual cornucopia of transitions without name could be seen in the 1994–95 season of the television sitcom *Home Improvement.* When a film or *videotape* has been developed or processed, edited, and *put in the can* (all its reels put into containers), it is ready for duplication and distribution to theaters.

FILM PROJECTION SPEED. The rapidity at which a reel of film is played. See *camera techniques.*

FILM SPEED. The relative ability of film to require amounts of light. Fast film requires little light to take an image; slow speed requires more. Generally, fast film is for indoor shots, and slower film is for outdoor photography.

FILMSCRIPT. The *scenario* or text for a *screenplay.*

FLIES. An area above the stage of a theater where various equipment is located, including overhead lights, equipment for the raising and lowering of *backdrops* and *sets,* and specialized gear such as that required to introduce the *deus ex machina* onto the stage, as, for instance, when Peter Pan flies onstage. In brief, the overhead stage space of a *theater.*

FLOODLIGHT. Intense *lighting,* such as is used in cinema and television photography.

FOIL. A *straight man*, often called the *second banana*, who stands opposite the comedian in a stage act and is the brunt of or helps set up the jokes. George Burns was Gracie Allen's straight man.

FOLK PLAY. Any play of unknown origin, generally performed annually, or at any rate regularly, as a ritual tradition; occasionally, like the medieval French *Play of Daniel*, discovered through archival research or reconstructed, as in the case of *The Book of Job,* which has been restored in the twentieth century as a Greek tragedy (q.v.) in chapter text. See also, *liturgical drama.*

FOOTLIGHTS. The illuminations that used to line the lip of a *stage*. See *lighting.*

FORESHADOWING. A hint of things to come; see *movement.*

FORWARD. Anything that helps a plot to advance; see *movement.*

FOURTH WALL. The front of a box *set* facing the audience.

FRAME, FREEZE, FREEZE FRAME. A single photograph (also called a *still*) in a film. See *camera angles* and *film editing.*

FURNITURE. The *props* that are used in a *set.*

GAGLINE. A humorous bit of dialogue.

GENRE. Type, or kind, of literature. Drama is a literary genre; subgenres of drama include tragedy, comedy, liturgical drama, and so forth.

HAMARTIA. The classical Greek term for the tragic flaw (q.v. in text above).

HANGING ENDING. An ambiguous conclusion of a story or drama. See *ending.*

HARLEQUINADE. A comic stage performance in which the clown Harlequin is the leading character or, in general, a clown drama or *entr'acte.* See also *mummery, pantomime.*

HEROIC DRAMA. The overblown drama of the English Restoration, having to do with larger-than-life protagonists, members of the nobility or royalty, who performed superhuman deeds in the name of honor and love.

HIGH COMEDY. Plays in which the airs, morals, and snobbery of the upper classes is satirized, as in the *comedy of manners*; or plays in which there is much banter among the personae (*repartee*) and witty *one-liners* (the *bon mot*) but little action, as in the *comedy of wit* of the *Restoration theater* that followed the return of the monarchy in England in the seventeenth century. Such a play set in the single scene of the withdrawing room is called a *drawing room comedy*.

HIGH-ANGLE SHOT. A photograph from a high *camera angle*.

HISTORY PLAY. A synonym for *chronicle play*. In the English Renaissance, a play derived from *Holinshed's Chronicles* or other histories.

HORSE OPERA. A cowboy movie or serial; see *oater, melodrama*, and *western*.

IMPROVISATIONAL THEATER. Off-the-cuff theatrical entertainments, generally of the comic variety; spontaneous *comedies*.

INCIDENTAL MUSIC. Music composed to accompany certain scenes or acts in a play that does not otherwise use music as an integral part of the performance, for instance, cinema scores.

INGÉNUE. A young female character, innocent and inexperienced. See *melodrama*.

IN MEDIAS RES. Beginning a story "in the center of the action"; see *point of attack*.

INTELLECTUAL DRAMA. A theater piece in which theme is of more importance than plot, character, or action; an idea play, such as those written by Henrik Ibsen and George Bernard Shaw. *The Wild Duck* is an example by the former; *Major Barbara,* by the latter. See *problem play*.

INTERLOCUTOR. The questioner in an *interview*. Also, the emcee, or master of ceremonies, of a *minstrel* show or *blackface* revue who stands between the two end-men of the chorus with whom he exchanges quips and jokes.

INTERLUDE. A short performance such as a ballet, a pantomime, a tableau, or an *entr'acte* that is staged between the acts of a longer drama.

INTERVIEW. A conversation between two people, one of whom is the subject and the other the questioner, or *interlocutor*.

INTRUSION. Something forcing its way into the play that shatters the *stasis* and changes everything from that point forward; it can be something physical, or it can be a *recognition* of something, such as the nature of the situation or of one's own character. Opposing forces renew the conflict until stasis is reestablished at the conclusion of the play if it has a *resolution;* if it does not, then the ending will hang ambiguously, it will be *open-ended* rather than closed.

INVIDIA. The classical Greek term for envy.

IRIS. A *film editing* technique in which a succeeding scene appears as a central insert on the screen and expands until it has forced the previous scene out of the edges of the picture.

JESTER. A comic character, such as Harlequin, in a clown drama.

JOKE LINE. A line of humorous dialogue in a theatrical performance.

KABUKI PLAY. A Japanese drama similar to the *noh play.* However, it is less formal and ritualized, more eclectic in its use of narrative, dance, acrobatics, and music from various sources, many of them traditional.

KINESCOPE. In early television, a film made of a live transmission. It was replaced by *videotape.*

LAZZI. Jokes, "material," stage business. See *comedies.*

LEADING LADY, LEADING MAN. The female or male lead in a dramatic performance; see *dramatis personae.*

LEGITIMATE THEATER. A term used to distinguish drama enacted live before a live audience in a theater from non-live presentations, as in cinema or on television, or from lesser theatrical productions.

LIBRETTO. The text for a musical play of some sort, such as an opera or operetta

LIGHTING. The illumination of a stage. The *footlights* were the illuminations that lined the *lip* of the proscenium, but there are various other kinds of lights in the modern theater, including *spotlights,* which are at times directed to illuminate specific actors, and *backlights,* which illuminate actors from behind so as to throw them into silhouette, sometimes against a *scrim.*

LIGHT OPERA (*comic opera, opéra bouffe, opera buffa, operetta*). As the terms suggest, humorous or satirical opera that contains all the elements of opera except, sometimes, *recitative.*

LIP. The front edge of a stage, separating it from the orchestra.

LITTLE THEATER. Noncommercial in character and often experimental, the "little theater" can be located nearly anywhere, in any city or village.

LITURGICAL DRAMA. Forms of liturgical drama, that is, plays written to be performed in the church or as part of a religious ritual, include the *morality play,* which is a medieval verse or compound-mode *allegory* (q.v.) in dramatic form. It rehearses the pilgrimage of man's progress toward death and his hope of salvation from sin through repentance and submission to God's mercy. Other than the pilgrimage, the elements are the *psychomachia,* or strife of the Seven Deadly Sins, aided by the Vices, with the Four Cardinal and Three Theological Virtues over possession of Everyman's soul; and the totentanz, or Dance of Death. Besides Death, other *personified abstractions* are Conscience, Conviction of Sin, and Repentance. Three other medieval liturgical plays are the *miracle play,* which depicts Bible stories or the lives of the saints; the *mystery play,* which is based upon the biblical story of humanity's Creation, Fall, and Redemption; and the *passion play,* which deals with the events in the life of Christ before the Resurrection, between the Last Supper and the Crucifixion.

LOBBY. The room or hall that serves as the entranceway to a *theater.*

LONG SHOT. A distant *camera angle.*

LOW COMEDY. Vulgar *comedies.*

LOW-ANGLE SHOT. A *camera angle* from below the subject.

LYRIC TRAGEDY. A form of *opera* popular during the reign of Louis XIV (1638–1715) that mixed song and spectacle (special effects). A modern version is *La Voix Humane* by Francis Poulenc (1899–1963), in which the special effects were provided by the recent technical innovation, the telephone. A *mock-lyric tragedy* is William Schuman's *The Mighty Casey*.

MAIN ACTION. The primary conflict in a drama; see *point of attack*.

MAIN FEATURE. A play or other dramatic production that is the featured attraction of the performance; it may include shorter productions such as a *curtain raiser*, *plampede*, or *entr'acte*.

MANLY HERO. The protagonist of a *melodrama*.

MASK, MASQUE. A relatively short verse or compound-mode drama dating from the Renaissance, performed by masked figures. It includes song, speeches, dance, *mime* (*pantomime*, *mummery*), *tableau* (freeze-scene), and *spectacle* (lavish display) and was a forerunner of *opera*. Contemporary masques are largely literary rather than dramatic (see *closet drama*). E. E. Cummings (1894–1962) wrote masques, among them one titled "Santa Claus," and Robert Frost (1874–1963) wrote some as well.

In the seventeenth century, Ben Jonson wrote many masques and *antimasques*, which were largely choreographed dances by *mummers*, that is, professional actors dressed in hideous and repulsive masks and costumes. These grotesques were subdued and banished by the courtly *amateur players* for whom the production was mounted. See *disguisings*.

MATERIAL. Another word for the jokes or gags of a comedian; see *lazzi*.

MATINEE. The daytime showing of a cinematic or theatrical production.

MATINEE IDOL. Usually a male star who, in romantic productions, is able to draw the adult female audience into the theaters. See *comedies* and *comedy of humours*.

MEDIUM SHOT. A *camera angle* that shows a subject in its surroundings, not closeup or at a considerable distance.

MELODRAMA. Any stage production, movie, radio play or television drama (*soap opera*, *sitcom* [situation comedy], or *oater*, i.e., western "*horse opera*") that uses *stereotypes*: characters who are two-dimensional and representative not of individual personalities so much as classes or kinds of people, for instance, the *villain* or the evil *antagonist*, the *ingenue* or innocent maiden, and the *boyish* or *manly hero* who often rescues the maiden from the clutches of the villain. Melodramas also typically employ the depiction of exaggerated emotions (*emoting*) and of overblown conflicts, and often they depict middle-class characters and situations, in which case they are examples of *bourgeois drama*. *Serial melodramas*, such as those that were once shown in movie theaters, were called *cliffhangers* because each *episode* ended with the hero or heroine poised to be dashed over a cliff or about to meet some other perilous end; the succeeding episode would begin at that *turning point* (*plot point*) and would end the *suspense* by showing how the protagonist had been saved from a *fate* (that was sometimes) worse than death.

METADRAMA. Drama about drama, such as Pirandello's *Six Characters in Search of an Author*, discussed in the introductory essay of this chapter. (See *metafiction*, *metanonfiction*, and metapoetry in *The Book of Forms*).

MEZZANINE. The lower balcony of a *theater* or the first row or two of a balcony.

MIDPOINT. The halfway mark of a *screenplay*.

MILES GLORIOSUS. A character in a *comedy of humours*.

MIME. Originally, the portrayal on stage of well-known situations and characters by means of farce, mockery, coarse dialogue, and mummery. In the modern sense, mime is acting without words, in gestures and actions only, *pantomime*.

MINSTREL SHOW. The American minstrel show was, during the nineteenth century, a *burlesque* in *blackface*: White men (not women) were made up to look like caricatures of people of color. Al Jolson carried the tradition into the twentieth century. For some of the personnel of the minstrel show, see *interlocutor*.

MIRACLE PLAY. A *liturgical drama* that depicts Bible stories or the lives of the saints.

MISE EN SCÈNE. The *setting* or *set* of a play, including the arrangement of all actors and props.

MOCK-LYRIC TRAGEDY. A take-off on a *lyric tragedy*.

MONOLOG, MONOLOGUE. A passage spoken by a lone actor on a stage. See also *soliloquy*.

MORALITY PLAY. A *liturgical drama* that rehearses the pilgrimage of man's progress toward death and his hope of salvation from sin through repentance and submission to God's mercy.

MOTION PICTURES. Movies, the *cinema*.

MOUNTING. Producing a play.

MOUTHPIECE. A character in a play who speaks for the author; see *dramatis personae*.

MOVEMENT. The pace of the action of the play. A *forward* is anything at all that moves the plot ahead, whether an action performed by a character; a *foreshadowing,* or hint, of things to come; or a *setup* of some kind, for instance, a character picking up an object and handling it seemingly at random but drawing attention to it thereby; when, later on, it becomes important, the audience will remember its significance.

MOVIES, MOVING PICTURES. See *cinema*.

MUMMER. A comic actor wearing a *mask*. See *mummery* and *masque*.

MUMMERY. Comic or satirical performances by actors wearing masks.

MUSICAL, MUSICAL COMEDY. The term "musical'"' is nowadays applied to the American or British musical plays, sometimes referred to as *Broadway musicals*. These productions are often *extravaganzas* and nearly always humorous except in such crossbreeds as Leonard Bernstein's *West Side Story*.

MUSICAL PLAY, MUSICAL THEATER. Any theatrical performance that requires song and dance, such as the *Broadway musical, light opera, lyric tragedy, opera*, and *vaudeville*.

MYSTERY PLAY. A *liturgical drama* based on the biblical story of humanity's Creation, Fall, and Redemption.

NARRATOR. One who tells a story. See *film editing* and *interview*.

NEW WAVE (*nouvelle vague*). An early 1960s film style similar to *cinema verité*, utilizing various techniques that gave the viewer a sense of both the chaotic nature of existence and the personality of the *auteur*.

NOH PLAY. A classical Japanese *compound-mode* drama, somewhat similar to the *masque* and to tragedy. It is allusive and impressionistic. It uses traditional subjects, masked figures, a *chorus*, *pantomime* (or *dumb show*), music, and *choreographed movement*. The Modernist Irish poet William Butler Yeats wrote plays that were influenced by the noh.

NOUVELLE VAGUE. French for *new wave*.

NUNTIUS. The messenger to the protagonist of a classical tragedy who recognizes in the message his impending doom.

OATER. A *western*; see also *melodrama*.

OBLIGATORY SCENE. Also called a *scène à faire*, it is one that is so obviously called for by the plot of a *well-made play* that the playwright is obliged to write it.

OFF-BROADWAY. Theater that is nearly as good as Broadway, at least as far as prestige goes, though the theaters in Greenwich Village and Soho in New York are generally smaller houses.

OFFSTAGE. The areas of a theater, including *backstage*, which is the area of the theater behind the stage, and the *wings*, the areas to the right and left of the performing area.

ONE-LINER. A joke told in a single breath: "Women are wonderful—take my wife. Please!"

OPEN-ENDED. An inconclusive or ambiguous ending of a story or drama.

OPERA. Classical *musical theater* consisting of *recitative*, which is dialogue declaimed, half-sung; *arias*, which are solos; *duets*, *trios*, *quartets*, and so forth; *choruses;* and various groupings of singers up to and including the entire cast in *ensemble* performance.

OPÉRA BOUFFE (French), OPERA BUFFA (Italian), OPERETTA (English). See *light opera*.

OPPOSITION. That which stands against a protagonist. See *dramatic situation*.

OPSIS. The classical Greek term for *spectacle*.

ORCHESTRA. The area below the lip of a proscenium stage, where the musicians are situated, or that portion of the auditorium closest to the musicians.

OUTLINE. The *scenario* of a stage or film story.

PAN. A bad review of a dramatic production. See also *camera angles*.

PANTOMIME. Acting with silent gestures. See *masque* and *noh play*.

PANTOMIMIST. One who writes pantomimes.

PARABASIS. The classical Greek term for the *aside*.

PARADIGM. The model of something, in particular, in this context, a *screenplay*.

PASSION PLAY. A *liturgical drama* that deals with the events in the life of Christ before the Resurrection, between the Last Supper and the Crucifixion.

PASTORAL DRAMA. A sort of expanded dramatic eclogue (see *The Book of Forms*). Practitioners in England were Samuel Daniel (1562?–1619), John Fletcher (1579–1625), and Ben Jonson. Set in the countryside, they featured rural characters such as shepherds and shepherdesses, idyllic scenes, and simple themes.

PATHOS. The classical Greek term for pity or sympathy.

PATTER SONG. A particular feature of English light opera, witty, clever, and delivered at high speed, "trippingly on the tongue," as in the operettas of Gilbert and Sullivan.

PERIPETEIA. The classical Greek term for peripety meaning a sudden reversal of fortune.

PERSONIFIED ABSTRACTIONS. Allegorical representations of ideas or qualities, for instance, evil represented by a type of human being or demon or love represented by a naked infant or cherub. See *liturgical drama*.

PICTURE–FRAME STAGE. A *proscenium* stage.

PIÈCE À THÈSE. The French term for *problem play*.

PIÈCE BIEN FAITE. The French term for *well-made play*.

PILOT. A television production made on speculation as a test vehicle for a projected TV series.

PIT. The area beneath the lip of the proscenium stage where the musicians are located. For another definition, see *theater*.

PLAMPEDE. A theatrical diversion or *entr'acte*.

PLATFORM. The main area of a proscenium stage. See *theater*.

PLAY TO THE PIT. In theater, to aim at reaching the lowest common denominator of the audience. See *theater*.

PLAYWRIGHT. The author of a play.

PLOT. The series of related rising actions leading to the *climax* in a written or theatrical narrative; the thread of associated incidents that makes a story, including its beginning, middle, and end.

PLOT POINT. A turning point in the plot of a *screenplay*.

POINT OF ATTACK. That instant in a play when the *main action* of the plot begins, often *in medias res*, in the middle of the main action.

PRATFALL. A deliberate comic error by an actor in a comedy or *farce*; *slapstick*.

PRAXIS. The classical Greek term for *action*.

PROBLEM PLAY. Also *thesis play* (*pièce à thèse*), such as was written by Henrik Ibsen or George Bernard Shaw; an *intellectual drama* that posed a contemporary problem and then explored, largely through dialogue rather than action, various possible solutions to the problem. Such a play would correspond in theater with the thematic story of fiction, for character, plot, and atmosphere are subordinated to the manipulation of ideas. Its predecessor was the French *drame*, a *disquisitory drama* written to display the interaction of ideas through dialogue. Often such a play is better read than enacted as, for instance, the section of George Bernard Shaw's *Man and Superman* titled "Don Juan in Hell."

PRODUCER. The person who finds the money to back the production of a play or film and supervises it financially.

PRODUCTION. See *backstage* and *property*.

PROPERTY. A play or other dramatic production that is owned by or optioned to a producer. See also *stage properties*.

PROPS. Stage properties; see *set* and *setting*.

PROSCENIA. The plural of *proscenium*. In Greek classic theater proscenia denoted the buildings in back of the stage.

PROSCENIUM. That portion of the stage located between the curtain and the orchestra.

PROSCENIUM ARCH. The frame of a proscenium or "picture frame" stage from which the curtain depends.

PROTAGONIST. The main character of a story; see *dramatic situation*, *dramatis personae,* and discussion of tragedy in text.

PSYCHOMACHIA. The strife of the Seven Deadly Sins, aided by the Vices, with the Four Cardinal and Three Theological Virtues over possession of Everyman's soul; see *liturgical drama*.

PUNCH AND JUDY SHOW. A traditional kind of *puppet play* starring these two characters, who hit each other with bats; see *farce* and *slapstick*.

PUPPET PLAY. A *farce* or other children's entertainment featuring movable dolls manipulated by a puppeteer behind the scenes.

PUT IN THE CAN. Finish a cinema; see *film editing*.

QUARTET. A four-part song; see *opera*.

RADIO. An aural broadcast medium.

RADIO PLAY. A drama written to be performed on radio and to be heard only, not seen (see *closet drama*).

RAISONNEUR. A "chorus character," one who performs the function of a Greek chorus in that he or she comments on the action of the play, sometimes speaking as a *surrogate* (*stand-in*, *mouthpiece*) for the author and acting like the omniscient or ironical narrator of a Victorian novel.

RECITATIVE. Speech in an *opera* that is not quite song.

RECOGNITION, RECOGNITION SCENE. That point in a tragedy or other play when the protagonist for the first time understands the consequences of his or her past actions or present situation. See *intrusion*.

REEL. A spool of film.

REGIONAL THEATER. A mixture of amateur casts headed at times by one or two professional leading actors.

REPARTEE. Rapid, witty dialogue in which one speaker attempts to outdo the other. See *high comedy*.

REPERTOIRE. The stock of plays kept current by a *repertory theater*.

REPERTORY THEATER. A theater company that keeps a backlist of plays that can be called to active production periodically; this stock is called its *repertoire*, a word that also signifies the plays or musical productions an actor or singer has committed to memory.

RESOLUTION. The wrapping up of the plot of a story or drama; see *denouement* and *intrusion*.

RESTORATION THEATER. The revival of the proscribed drama in Great Britain after the Puritan interregnum and during the restored monarchy in 1660. See *high comedy*.

REVENGE TRAGEDY. An Elizabethan tragedy that contained elements similar to those of the *chronicle play* and usually concerned itself with the protagonist's pursuit of vengeance for the loss of a loved one.

REVUE. A *musical* entertainment made up of skits, songs, and dances, sometimes related thematically but often not, containing elements of satire, extravaganza, and spectacle.

ROGUE COMEDY. A satirical play that has as its protagonist a lovable rascal, like Ben Jonson's *Alchemist*.

ROLE. A dramatic character part assigned to an *actor* or *actress* who is a member of the *cast* (*dramatis personae*) of a play.

ROLL. A continuous film sequence; see *camera techniques*.

ROMANTIC COMEDY. A modern play that is similar to the New Comedy of Menander, discussed in the text. An example would be Shakespeare's *As You Like It*, which is set in the utopia of the Forest of Arden in which the young lovers meet with many a mishap before they are united.

ROMANTIC TRAGEDY. Any nonclassical form of tragedy, the invention of such twentieth-century playwrights as Arthur Miller (b. 1915), Eugene O'Neill (1888–1953), and Tennessee Williams (1911–83) whose plays show the "tragedy" inherent in the everyday lives of ordinary people.

SATYR PLAY. An ancient Greek dramatic performance that was ribald, satirical, and slapstick. It was performed after every third tragedy enacted in a competition to provide relief for the tensions that had been building up in the audience throughout the performances.

SCAPEGOAT. A "sacrificial lamb," someone who is blamed for the offenses of others. It has been argued that the hero of a tragedy is in fact the scapegoat or "ritual victim" a society demands as a sacrifice for its own sins.

SCENARIO. The broad *outline* of the plot of a play or story, giving general descriptions of characters and events but not containing details. An outline summarizes the proposed narrative in five to fifteen pages, whereas a *treatment* is from fifteen to thirty pages in length and contains more detail, including illustrations of dialogue. The term also may denote a completed *filmscript* or *screenplay* for *cinema* or *teleplay* for *television*.

SCENE. A scene is a lesser unit of the drama than an act; either it specifies a locale or time different from the previous or succeeding locale or *setting*, or it signifies a particular group of actors and actresses on the stage. In this latter sense, if there is even a partial change of *cast* (see *dramatis personae*), a new scene takes place. A third meaning of "scene" is nearly synonymous with *setting* or *set*, as in the term scenery, which depicts the arrangement of the *properties* (*props* for short) on the *stage*, including such things as *backdrops*, *lighting,* and other *stage effects* and items of *stage business* and *stagecraft*.

SCÈNE À FAIRE. The French form of *obligatory scene*.

SCENE DROP. A kind of *curtain,* located behind the main curtain, a drape that falls to indicate a scene shift or a new act.

SCHOOL PLAY. A synonym for *academic drama*.

SCREENPLAY. A drama written for cinema or television. See *scenario*. The *paradigm* of the screenplay is generally three acts long, with a beginning, a middle, and an end. Act 1 is the beginning (about thirty minutes), and it opens with the *setup* (exposition). At the end of the first act there is the first *plot point*, a *turning point* in the plot that aims the audience toward the second act. Act 2 is the middle of the screenplay, and it is twice as long as the first or third act (sixty minutes); it is broken into two halves, at the center of which is the *midpoint* or *crisis*. The first half rises to the midpoint, and the second half falls—through the *black moment*, when all looks lost for the protagonist in his or her attempt to achieve the goal—to the second plot point (*climax*) at the end of act 2, which aims the audience toward the third act. Act 3 (thirty minutes or less) is the *resolution* of the screenplay.

SCRIM. A fabric curtain or *backdrop* or *backcloth* that is either transparent or opaque, depending on the direction of the lighting: if the lighting is from the front, it is opaque.

SCRIPT. Any written *drama*, *filmscript*, *radio play*, *screenplay*, or *teleplay*.

SECOND BANANA. The *foil* or *straight man* of a comedian.

SENEX, SENEX IRATUS. A member of the *dramatis personae* of a *comedy of humours*.

SERIAL MELODRAMA. A *melodrama* performed or filmed in episodes.

SET. The physical layout of the stage, including all props and backdrops. A *box set* is the stage laid out so as to depict a room with three walls, two at the sides and one at the rear, the *fourth wall* being a *cutaway*—either imagined as separating the audience from the play or with a net of *scrim* (loosely woven fabric) through which the audience can see if and when the lighting permits.

SET PIECE. A set piece is an artistically formal scene or play, or it is a formula play.

SETTING. The place where a *scene* takes place.

SETUP. Something earlier in a play that prepares the audience for a succeeding action or situation. See *movement* and *screenplay*.

SHOT. A photograph; see *camera techniques*.

SHOWBOAT. A floating *theater*.

SILVER SCREEN. The surface on which a moving picture is shown; also a synonym for *cinema* itself.

SITCOM. A television *situation comedy*.

SITUATION COMEDY. Generally a half-hour *teleplay*. See *melodrama* and *television*.

SLAPSTICK. Crude physical humor; the bat used by Punch and Judy; see *puppet play* and *farce*.

SLOMO. Slow motion; see *camera techniques*.

SLOW FILM. A photographic surface that requires much light; see *camera techniques*.

SLOW MOTION. Running developed motion picture film at a speed slower than that at which the pictures were taken; see *camera techniques*.

SMALL SCREEN. Television, in contrast to the *big* or *silver screen*, which is *cinema*.

SOAP OPERA. A synonym for *melodrama*.

SOCKS. Part of the wardrobe of the classical Greek actor; see *buskins*.

SOFT FOCUS. A slightly out of focus shot or one taken through a filter; see *camera angles*.

SOLILOQUY. A passage spoken by a lone actor onstage. It differs from the *monologue*, which assumes an audience, in that it is the character's private thoughts verbalized and spoken aloud.

SPEAR–BEARER. In *opera,* a minor nonspeaking character, such as a guard at the palace door. Often such people are members of the chorus.

SPECIAL EFFECTS. Camera, digital, electronic, and mechanical techniques that simulate scenes and actions. See *spectacle*.

SPECTACLE. Stage effects of all sorts. See *lyric tragedy* and *masque*.

SPOTLIGHT. Pinpoint *lighting* on a stage that picks out a particular actor or object.

S.R.O. **S**tanding **R**oom **O**nly.

STAGE. An area reserved for public performance of drama. The stage proper is the area between the *curtain* and the rear wall of a *proscenium*.

STAGE BUSINESS. An action onstage by a member of the cast to fill in a pause in the dialogue, to fill in a detail of the story, or to set up a later scene or action. See also *comedies* and *scene*.

STAGECRAFT. Theatrical skill. See *scene*.

STAGE EFFECT. Something created onstage that makes a particular impression, for instance, a mist or the ringing of a bell. See *scene*, *special effects*, and *spectacle*.

STAGE LEFT, STAGE RIGHT. The areas of the stage to the left and right respectively, as the actors face the audience.

STAGE MANAGER. The person in charge of *props*, *lighting*, and the technical aspects of the drama being produced, See *props*.

STAGE PROPERTIES. "Props." See *scene*.

STALLS. The seats closest to the stage, nearest the orchestra *pit*. See *theater*.

STAND–IN. A character in a play who speaks for the author; see *dramatis personae* and *mouthpiece*.

STAR. The most famous member of the cast of a play or moving picture, male or female, whose reputation and drawing power—in and of themselves, regardless of the strength of the production—are sufficient to bring an audience into the theater.

STARLET. A rising female actress in her first few featured roles.

STASIS. The point at which there is no movement, when opposing forces strike a *balance,* and *tension* and *suspense* build.

STILL. One frame in a moving picture; a single photograph; see *camera angles* and *film editing.*

STRAIGHT CUT. An abrupt transition from one scene to another in a moving picture. See *film editing.*

STRAIGHT MAN. The *foil* or *second banana* of a comedian.

STRONG CURTAIN. A particularly effective ending for a play or a single act.

STYLIZED CHARACTER. A traditional role in a particular type of play; a stereotype of a historical or mythological figure. See *dramatis personae* and *typecasting.*

SUMMER THEATER. Located in regions where tourism thrives, it frequently does the same.

SURROGATE. A character in a play who speaks for the author, a *mouthpiece* or *stand-in.* See *dramatis personae.*

SUSPENSE. Tension in a story or drama. See *melodrama* and *stasis.*

TABLEAU. A "freeze-scene" executed by real people who depict onstage what amounts to a living sculpture; see *masque.*

TECHNOFANTASY. *Science fiction* or fantasy cinema that relies on *special effects.*

TEEVEE. Shorthand for *television;* also, TV and, in England, *telly.*

TELEPLAY. A *screenplay* written for television. The paradigm of the two-hour *feature television script* will be somewhat different, although it too will have a beginning, a middle, and an end; these, however, will be broken into seven *acts,* each from about eight to fourteen minutes in length to accommodate *commercial messages* but none to end exactly on the half-hour. Each act should end at a plot point of some kind to aim the audience forward into the next act over the commercials. The *comedy script* should be 95 to 115 pages in length; the *dramatic script*, 105 to 125 pages long, one page being approximately equivalent to one minute. The one-hour script will be about 60 pages long and consist of four acts, each approximately a quarter-hour long.

TELEVISION. A visual broadcast medium.

TELEVISION SCRIPT. A *teleplay*.

TELLY. British equivalent of *teevee* or TV; that is, *television*.

TENSION. The equilibrium established in a play when opposing forces are of equal strangth; see *stasis*.

THEATER, THEATRE. The staging of a play is occasionally in an *arena theater,* sometimes called *theater in the round*, which has no *proscenium* but is surrounded by the audience, through which the actors must walk to reach the cleared area, or *platform,* where the play is being enacted. Other sorts of theatrical spaces include the *amphitheater*, in which the seats for the audience rise in tiers above the playing area; the *auditorium*, a large, generalized building or room in a public building; the *showboat*, which caters to the river towns and contains a theater; and the *dinner theater,* which is a restaurant equipped to present a theatrical entertainment after the meal.

The bottom floor of a theater that contains more than one level for the audience is called the *orchestra*, and the seats closest to the stage, nearest the orchestra *pit*, are called the *stalls*; confusingly, the British call the area beyond the stalls the *pit,* which, in Shakespeare's time, commanded the cheapest ticket prices and thus attracted the least prepossessing *theatergoers*. It was necessary for playwrights to *play to the pit* or suffer the displeasure of the mob. The level above the orchestra is the *mezzanine,* which is often flanked by the private *boxes*, and the level above these is the *balcony*. If all seats are filled for a performance, a sign in the *lobby* of the theater near the *box office* will usually proclaim that there is S.R.O. which indicates "Standing Room Only."

THEATERGOERS. Playgoers; the audience for plays.

THEATER-IN-THE-ROUND. *Arena theater*.

THEATRE DISTRICT. The area of London where most of the theaters are located.

THESIS PLAY. A synonym for *problem play*.

THESPIAN. An actor or actress; from Thespis, the inventor of the Greek tragedy.

TILT SHOT. A photograph from above or below. See *camera angles*.

TOTENTANZ. The dance of death in a *morality play*.

TRACKING SHOT. A moving picture photograph that follows a moving object; see *camera angles*.

TRAGICOMEDY. A relatively short verse or *compound-mode* (verse and prose) drama combining tragedy and comedy, usually in a *complication* (plot–subplot) relationship. Good is rewarded and vice punished.

TRANSLATION. The rendering of a literary work written in one language into another language.

TRANSLATOR. One who makes translations; in theater, a *dramaturge*.

TRAVELING SHOT. A synonym for *tracking shot*. See *camera angles*.

TREATMENT. A *scenario* that contains more information than an outline but less than a full script.

TRIO. A three-part song in an *opera*.

TRITAGONIST. The third most important character in a tragedy; see *dramatis personae*.

TURNING POINT. The point at which the plot veers in another direction. See *melodrama* and *screenplay*.

TV. *Television, teevee, telly.*

TYPECASTING. To cast an actor in a role to which he or she appears to be suited by personality or appearance or to cast an actor in the same kind of role over and over again. See *dramatis personae*.

UNDERSTUDY. To prepare to replace another actor or actress; a person who does so.

UPSTAGE. Deliberate overshadowing of one actor by another. Also, upstage is that portion of the stage farthest from the audience and in fact was at one time the highest portion of the stage, which was tilted downward for easier viewing.

VAUDEVILLE. *Musical theater* that consists of skits, revues, stand-up comedy routines, song-and-dance acts, and so forth; a melange of brief acts.

VIDEOTAPE. The magnetic medium on which television programs are directly recorded and films are transcribed for home viewing, replacing the *kinescope*. See *film editing*.

VILLAIN. The antagonist of a *melodrama*.

VOICE-OVER. See *dubbing*.

VOX POPULI. The voice of the people, represented in a tragedy by the *chorus*. See *dramatis personae*.

WALK-ONS. Minor characters generally without lines, who on occasion may, however, have a line or two; for instance, the butler who enters the library of the mansion and announces: "Dinner is served."

WELL-MADE PLAY (*pièce bien faite*). A play that displays the same qualities as the well-made story (q.v., preceding chapter).

WINDOW STAGE. Traditionally, plays are performed on a window stage or *picture-frame stage* that is separate from and raised above the audience and has a *proscenium*.

WINGS. The wings are the areas to the right and left of the *stage*.

WIPE. A film transition in which one scene takes over the screen from the left or right as the old scene is wiped off it. See *film editing*.

ZOOM SHOT. A photograph made while moving the camera in a rush either away from or toward the object on which it is focusing. See *camera angles*.

The Genres of Nonfiction

"Nonfiction" is a catch-all term encompassing many subgenres. The *formal essay* is a scholarly *disquisition* on a particular subject, whereas the *informal essay* is a *discussion* of some topic in a less rigorous vein. *Criticism*, including the short form called the *review* or *critique*, is commentary on art, music, literature, drama, dance, and other forms of creative endeavor; *history* is writing on the past; and *speculation* is writing about the possibilities of the future. *Professional writing* is a category encompassing such subgenres as *technical writing* (manuals, articles on medical techniques), *business writing* (letters, merchandising and manufacturing reports), and *report writing* of other kinds, for instance, a report from a field office to the home office regarding personnel matters.

Biography is the story of someone else's life; the *profile*, an essay-length biographical *character study*; *autobiography*, the story of one's own life; the *memoir*, a reminiscent essay. The *personal essay* is a discussion of some subject from the author's particular viewpoint; if the topic is a literary one and the style chatty and informal, it is a *causerie*.

The *journal* is a daily record of one's life, to be distinguished from *journalism*, which is *reportage* of current events for one of the *mass media* (singular, *medium*) including newspapers, radio, and television. Many terms from journalism are covered in entries in the chapter glossary, below.

A *Socratic dialogue* is a *didactic* work that follows the Platonic form of a conversation between teacher and student, such as Socrates is said to have conducted in the "Groves of Academe." *Letters* are *correspondence*, messages sent to other people, to be distinguished from *belles-lettres*, which means writing considered as an art form, pleasing to read in and of itself, like the work of Charles Lamb in his *Essays of Elia*. The writer of the *familiar essay*, which is written from but not necessarily entirely about one's own life, treats the reader as a confidante. The discussion is of a personal, visionary, or confessional nature, and it may move inward (*via negativa*), as in *The Confessions of Saint Augustine*, or outward (*via affirmativa*), as in *The Moon's a Balloon* by David Niven.

Other genres of literature, including fiction, drama, and poetry, are sometimes called the genres of "creative writing" or *writing arts*, but of recent years the term *creative nonfiction* has been deployed to indicate that certain nonfiction subgenres utilize many of the same "creative writing" techniques: *parafiction* is written as though it were a novel or short story, like the novel-cum-biography of Truman Capote (1924–84), *In Cold Blood; metanonfiction* is nonfiction about nonfiction. This article is itself an example of metanonfiction.

The reader who has been following this line of reasoning so far will have noticed two things: the speaker or *narrator* is conducting an *argument*; therefore, this is an *essay*. The essayist uses language as a bearer of argument or *information*, for there is a point to be proved or conveyed to the reader.

Kinds of Argument

There are two major kinds of *logical argument*. The first is *a priori*, beginning with a theory or *general principle* and proceeding to a specific conclusion in keeping with the *premises* that have been postulated: "Since all mortals die, and I am a mortal, I must die." The *syllogism* is a *form* of deductive reasoning that consists of a *major premise*, a *minor premise*, and a *conclusion*, as in "Grass is green," the major premise; "Bluegrass is grass," the minor premise; "Therefore, bluegrass is green," the conclusion. If the minor premise does not follow logically, then neither does the conclusion: "Bluegrass is blue; bluegrass is grass; therefore, grass is blue." A *categorical syllogism* addresses an entire classification (*taxonomy*) of things and is distinguished by the use of the words "every" or "all" in the major premise: "All men are unfeeling." *Differentia* are the distinguishing features existing between constituents of the same category: "Some men are unfeeling, but many are emotional to a fault." The *hypothetical syllogism* is conjectural, and it contains words such as "should," "if," "supposing," and so forth: "If dogs were the only animals that had fangs and wagging tails, and if Joe had fangs and a wagging tail, then Joe would be a dog." A *disjunctive syllogism* has to do with contradictions and oppositions, typified by the use of words such as "neither," "nor," "either," and "or": "Either men are unfeeling, or they are not; if they are not, then they are not men." An *enthymeme* is a syllogism that lacks or skips the minor premise: "All grass is green; therefore, bluegrass is green." *Tautology* is circular reasoning, vacuous repetition, or redundancy: "If it's going to rain tomorrow, then it's going to rain, and there's nothing one can do about it."

The second type of logical argument is *inductive reasoning,* which works in the opposite direction, deriving general principles from specific facts or examples: "These animals are no longer living, though once they were; they are mortal. Since these animals have died, as have others I have seen, it is likely that all animals are mortal and must die at last." *Empiricism* is the belief that only the experience of the senses can provide knowledge: "Seeing is believing" is an empirical *adage,* that is, a *proverb* or *old saw.* The scientific method is based on empiricism. *Textual support* is the body of *proofs* cited and adduced in defense of an argument. *Validity* has to do with judging the accuracy or truth of a well-reasoned argument.

Deduction and induction are arguments from *reason,* or *logos,* but other types of *artistic proofs* are by appeals to *ethos,* the good character and credibility of the speaker; *pathos,* the emotions; and *example* (*exemplum*; plural, *exempla*), the citation of an illustration of the argument. *Inartistic proofs*, which Aristotle said the rhetorician could also use to prove the argument are *laws*, *witnesses*, *contracts*, *oaths*, and *tortures*. All of these except the last continue to be used in courts of law.

Rhetoric

Rhetoric is the art of effective persuasion. Unfortunately, in modern times the term has fallen into disrepute. It has come to be used primarily in a pejorative sense to refer to bombastic language and pompous delivery, but rhetoric is a necessary and very useful tool in the modern world, just as it was in the ancient and medieval worlds. The debasement of the term appears to be the result of a modern Platonism, for Plato distrusted rhetoric on the grounds that, in his opinion, persuasion ought to take place directly and plainly, without artifice, through live dialogue. This view, which is itself a self-limiting *rhetorical doctrine*, was refuted by Artistotle; and the art of rhetoric was taught for centuries as an important element of a learned person's education, part of the *trivium,* which was the lower division of the seven liberal arts: *grammar,* the science of language systems; *logic* (specifically, *dialectic*), the science of rational argument through discourse; and *rhetoric*, the art of elocution and discourse. The upper division was the *quadrivium*, consisting of geometry, astronomy, arithmetic, and music.

Rhetoric is concerned with creating effects in the listener or reader, particularly in the sense of convincing him or her of the veracity of an *argument* (*logos*). Aristotle identified three types of rhetoric: *deliberative, judicial,* and *epideictic.* Deliberative, or *political, rhetoric* urges the audience to action; judicial, or *forensic, rhetoric* is an attack on or a defense of someone, and epideictic, or *ceremonial, rhetoric* praises or blames, as in a funeral eulogy.

The classical rhetorician believed that there were five considerations in the building of a discourse, three of them having to do with composition and two with performance: *invention,* or *heuresis,* the search for and discovery of arguments and proofs; *disposition,* or *taxis*, the way in which such materials were arranged and presented; *style*, or *elocution*, the manner in which the argument was conducted; *memory*, or *mneme*, the mental retention of subject matter, words, and arrangement; and *delivery*, or *hypocrisis*, the art of graceful and forceful public delivery.

Invention

The four basic elements of *expository writing* are the *subject* being examined; the *thesis*, or statement of the point the author is trying to prove; the *argument*, or backing, for the thesis, which consists of data and facts to serve as proof for the thesis; and the *conclusion*, or restatement of the proved thesis. There are two types of subject, according to Aristotle: *thesis*, or *general question* such as, "Ought all people to be kind to one another?" and *hypothesis*, or *specific question*: "Ought Elmer to be kind to his enemy Elmo?" One may be aided in the proper formation of a thesis by asking the questions *an sit*, "Does it exist?"; *quid sit*, "What is it?"; and *quale sit*, "What kind is it?"

Arrangement

The *subject*, or *topic* of discussion, which may be a word or a phrase, may be given as a *lemma* in the title, for example, "An Essay on Criticism" by Alexander Pope. Topics may be either special (*idioi topoi*) or common (*koinoi topoi*). *Division* separates elements of the topic into categories for clarity (*explanation*) and definition: "Our topic today is 'cats,' but we won't be speaking of the great cats, or even of wild cats, but of the common house cat." The *exordium* is the statement of the subject being examined and an introduction to the author's topic; it contains the *proposition* or *thesis sentence* (*partition*) of the discussion. It differs from the subject in that it must be expressed in a complete *statement*, that is to say, in an independent clause, not merely a phrase or dependent clause. Here is the first sentence of Alexander Pope's "An Essay on Criticism":

'Tis hard to say, if greater want of skill
Appear in writing or in judging ill;
But, of the two, less dang'rous is th' offence
To tire our patience, than mislead our sense.

[It is hard to say whether greater lack of skill
Appears in poor writing or in poor critical judgment;
But, of the two possibilities, the lesser offense
Is to tire the reader's patience rather than be obscure.]

The exordium is followed by the *narration*, which contains the *exposition,* or necessary background information, and the *definition of terms.* The argument proper is the amplification, or *proof,* which may be conducted in various ways. The proof has two parts, the first of which is the *confirmation*: the list of facts or data backing the thesis, usually arranged in the order of weakest argument to strongest (*climactic*). The second part of the argument is the *refutation*, the *rebuttal* of all possible arguments to the contrary, usually arranged in the order of strongest argument to weakest (*anticlimactic*). The *conclusion* consists, first, of a *summation* of the positive arguments and, second, of the *peroration*, which is an *appeal to emotion* as well as to logic, and the *restatement* of the *proved thesis.*

Style

The elements of style are four in number: *correctness,* or accuracy; *clarity,* or precision, of discussion; *appropriateness*, that is, the choice of style to suit the audience; and *ornament,* or graceful embellishment, of the discussion through the use of figures of speech such as metaphors and similes.

The essayist's techniques are primarily (though not absolutely) those of persuasion. Many people believe that, because the essayist is a "factual" writer, the argument will be based on *ratiocination,* or rational deduction, but this is not necessarily the case. In fact, argument may have as much to do with opinion as with observation, and an essayist may use as much passion as data—facts and figures—to support the argument. People may be as readily persuaded, if not more so, by such techniques as by coherence (intelligibility) and reason. It was this aspect of rhetoric that Plato objected to; see *rhetorical fallacies* in the chapter glossary, below.

However, if such is the situation—and it is, modern *advertising*, political *campaigning,* and *propaganda* being the worst offenders—the essayist must be prepared to answer in kind and to choose those techniques of logic **and** of rhetoric that will best enable him or her to win the argument; and the argument is won only when the reader is persuaded to the writer's view. The best essayists understand that, given the same argument written by two different writers, **the argument that is best written will generally be most persuasive**. Another way of saying this is "Style has as much to do with persuasion as anything else." Many stylists—graceful or forceful writers—who are poor logicians have won their arguments, and many a clear thinker has lost the battle.

George Puttenham (q.v., Bibliography) said the ancients set down six points that graceful writing ought to observe: (1) "decent proportion in writings and speech"; (2) "*sonority* and *musicality*"; (3) "neither overlengthiness nor underlengthiness, but proportionate to the purpose," called *syntomia* or *proportion*; (4) "orderly and good construction," called *synthesis* (see *schemes*); (5) "sound, proper, and natural speech," called *ciriologia* or grace of style, and (6) "liveliness," "appeal to the senses," called *tropus* (see *tropes*).

Rhetoricians distinguish among *high style*, meaning a grandiloquent manner of speaking; *mean style*, meaning a balanced manner of speaking; and *base* or *plain style*, meaning a vulgar manner of speaking. The modern critic Northrop Frye distinguished only between *demotic style*, a manner of speaking consistent with ordinary speech, and *hieratic style*, a self-consciously literary manner of speaking.

CHAPTER GLOSSARY
Italicized terms are glossed elsewhere in the book; see index.

ABECEDARIUS. A composition in prose or verse in which either each word of a stanza or sentence, beginning with **ay**, proceeds through the alphabet in order, like Geoffrey Chaucer's "A B C." Or all the words in each stanza or paragraph, from **ay** through **zed** (**zee**), begin with the same letter. See *didactics* and *primer* in *The Book of Forms*.

ABSTRACTION. Something that is incapable of conventional (not personal) definition; something that exists only if one believes it does. See *apostrophe*.

ACCISMUS. Refusal of something in a dissembling manner, hoping that the offer will be made again insistently: "I am unworthy of such an honor." It is a form of *irony*.

ACRONYM. A word made up of the first letters of words in a phrase: "snafu" = "**s**ituation **n**ormal, **a**ll **f**——ed **u**p."

AD. Short form of "advertisement." The British say "advert."

ADAGE. An old saw or wise saying; see *didactics, parimia,* and *sententia*.

AD HOMINEM. Verbal personal attack. See *rhetorical fallacies*.

ADJUNCTIO, ADJUNCTION. The addition of one thing to another, for instance, a syllable to a word, as in *proparalepsis*, or one term to another: "You, sir, are a gentleman and a scholar . . . and a good judge of cigars."

ADVERTISING. Drawing the attention of the buying public to a product.

ALLEGORICAL ALLUSION. See *ironical illusion*.

ALLEGORY. The discussion of abstractions in terms of actions, events, and personae, as in Aesop's fable "The Fox and the Grapes." This term is considered at some length in the chapter on "The Genres of Poetry" in our companion volume, *The Book of Forms: A Handbook of Poetics*.

ALLUSION. An indirect reference to something extraneous to the *argument* being conducted: "My opponent believes that he is the reincarnation of Julius Caesar. He'd better keep an eye out for his 'friend' Brutus."

ALPHABESTIARY. See *abecedarius* and also *bestiary* and *primer*.

AMBAGE. An ambiguious *riddle* or puzzle of some sort, a pun.

AMPHISBAENIA. Turning a word backward to make another word, as in "He **mined** ore dressed in **denim** jeans."

AMPLIFICATION. *Epenthis*, *proparalepsis*, *paragoge* and *prothesis* are *orthographical* (i.e., spelling) methods of expansion or proof of an argument.

ANACHINOSIS. Referring the reader, in an argument, to his own opinion: "If you don't believe me, figure it out for yourself."

ANACOLUTHON. A shift of grammatical construction in midsentence that leaves the beginning unfinished ("You may remember the night—. Listen! The dog is barking at the door").

ANADIPLOSIS. The linking of two consecutive clauses by a repetition of words: "I saw **her hair, her** dark **hair** windblown."

ANAGRAM. A word made by rearranging the letters of another word, for instance "stunted" instead of "student." See *metathesis*.

ANANTAPODATON. A synonym for *anacoluthon*.

ANAPHORA. The parallel repetition of an initial word in more than one sentence: "**Love** is many things. **Love** may be a many-splendored thing. **Love** on a cellar door, however, may be a many-splintered thing, as well."

ANATHEMA. Ritual *imprecation* directed by a religious body against a heretic.

ANASTROPHE. The inversion of normal syntax ("go I shall" for "I shall go").

ANECDOTE. A little story or allegory to illustrate a point, occasionally employed by an essayist.

ANGLE. The slant that a writer takes on a story. See *journalism*.

ANNOMINATION. Wordplay, as in the *pun*, the quibble, or the calembour. A synonym is *paronomasia*.

ANTANACLASIS. The witty repetition of a word in an amplified or changed sense—a *pun*. "What is the difference between an animal doctor and a former member of Hitler's army? One is a **veterinarian**, and the other is a **veteran Aryan**."

ANTENAGOGE. A statement made and then softened by the addition of a mitigating or less harsh alternative: "I wish that you'd fall over dead—well, maybe just fall down and knock your brains out."

ANTHIMERIA. One part of speech substituted for another; for instance, a noun for a verb as in "The clock's chime **belfries** above the city."

ANTICLIMAX. Working from the strongest to the weakest; its synonym is *meiosis*.

ANTIMETABOLE. The repetition of two beginning words, in reverse order, later in a sentence: "To **kiss her** is to love **her kiss**."

ANTIPHRASIS. Derision by means of simple *contrasts*; for instance, calling a fat person "skinny" or a thin one "fatso."

ANTIPOPHORA. Asking a question and then answering it oneself, as when a scarecrow asks the pumpkins in the field around him: "You worship me? a pole for a spine, a timber for my extended bone, fingers of hay stolen by wrens?" and then answers himself: "I bleach and shake, I shudder in the moon's dark. Pumpkins, crowd of orange globes, I whistle in the wind."

ANTISTHECON. A change in the sound of a word; for instance, "stoont" for "student."

ANTISTROPHE. The repetition of a single word throughout a written work.

ANTITHETON. The term describing the techniques of "the *devil's advocate*" in argument: taking any position and defending it simply in joy of the fight or to bring out some point that might otherwise remain unexamined.

ANTONOMASIA (*pronominatio*). Substituting for a noun a phrase describing the noun. The descriptive phrase (or epithet) is derived from some quality associated with the noun; for instance, instead of saying "Queen Elizabeth I," one might (and often does) say, "The Virgin Queen."

ANTONYM. A word that is opposite in meaning from another, as **hatred** is the antonym of **love**, and **down** is the antonym of **up**. See *antithetical parallelism* (in text), *constructional schemes,* and *paradiastole*.

APHAERESIS. A technique of overt *elision* that drops the initial unstressed syllable (usually a vowel) of a word (i.e., "'til" for "until," "'tis" for "it is," and "let's" for "let us."

APHORISM. A brief wise saying, an *adage*.

APOCOPE. A form of elision that drops syllables from the end of a word: "morn" for "morning."

APOLOGIA. A literary apology. See *metanoia* and *parisia*.

APOLOGUE. An animal fable with a moral point.

APOPHASIS. The rhetorical technique of denying one's intention to speak of a particular point, at the same time that one mentions it: "I don't intend to mention the fact that Mr. So-and-So was convicted of larceny."

APORIA. Expression of doubt or uncertainty: "if, in fact, one may ever be certain of anything."

APOSIOPESIS. Deletion of letters, syllables, words, or passages and substitution of some other symbol or symbols to take their place, as in the example of the *acronym*.

APOSTROPHE. Direct address, speaking to an absent human being or to a (usually) personified object or abstraction: "Hello, Mr. Tree, how are you this morning?"

APOTHEGM. A pithy, didactic saying, an adage; see *didactics* and *sententia*.

APPEAL TO AUTHORITY, TO FORCE, TO HUMOR, TO IGNORANCE, TO PITY, TO TRADITION. See *rhetorical fallacies*.

APPOSITION, APPOSITIVE. An equivalent noun inserted into a sentence to explain or expand on another noun: "My brother, GENE, is five years younger than I am." See *epitheton*.

ARA. A protracted ritual curse. See *imprecation*.

ARGUMENT. A discussion between people representing two sides of an issue. It is often conducted orally, and a formal oral argument is a debate.

ARTICLE. *Magazine journalism*. See *magazine*.

ARTICULATION (ARTICULUS). The clear sounding of each element of a unit of speech, such as each syllable in a word: "I do not for an **in-stant ex-pect** there to be a **di-mi-nu-tion** of **ig-no-rance** in my **op-po-nent**, so I will speak **clear-ly** in **or-der** that he may **un-der-stand**."

ASTEISMUS. Simple jesting, without rancor: "Did Samson Agonistes have the strength of twenty bulls at cowtime in the spring?"

ASYNDETON. The opposite of *polysyndeton*, the elimination of articles, conjunctions, and sometimes prepositions and pronouns from normal sentences ("I chased [the] wind, [the] wind chased me").

AUDIENCE. The vertical audience is that group of potential readers that exists at any given moment. Newspapers and newsmagazines are directed at this audience, which is vast. But the horizontal audience, which is that group of potential readers existing from any given moment forward into time, is even more vast. Thus, a poem may be printed in a little magazine today and be read by a vertical audience of only a thousand people. But if that poem is reprinted, first in a collection of the author's work and then in anthologies of poetry and literature and in textbooks used in school and university classes, as was the case with T. S. Eliot's *The Waste Land*, then the total number of readers of that poem will eventually greatly exceed the number of readers of any particular issue of *Time* magazine, a *mass circulation* weekly periodical. Reporters know they are writing for the readers of the moment; poets hope they are writing for the ages.

AUTHORIAL INTRUSION. A reader's sudden awareness of the author as a presence in the story. It may be in the form of *irony*.

AXIOM. An adage or old saw, a wise saying of received opinion. See *didactics*.

BAGATELLE. A witty or clever piece that utilizes such techniques as simple jesting; also called a *jeu d'esprit*.

BALANCE. See *comparison*. See also grammatical parallelism and parallel structure in text.

BANDWAGON FALLACY. See *rhetorical fallacies*.

BANTER. Verbal jousting. See *charientismus*.

BEAT. A term from journalism meaning the area of a reporter's expertise, for instance, "the police beat." See *editor* and *reporter*.

BESTIARY. A book of medieval fables concerning animals, both natural and mythical, used as allegories of human nature; the alphabestiary, a neologism coined by John Ciardi, signifies a modern alphabetical bestiary for children. See *didactics*.

BIAS. A leaning or prejudice that impairs objective judgement. See *rhetorical fallacies*.

BOMBAST. Verbal bullying, or *bomphiologia*.

BOMPHIOLOGIA. See preceding entry.

BRACHIOLOGA. The technique of separating words by pauses, usually indicated by means of punctuation (commas in particular) but sometimes typographically by means of spaces: "I said, hello!—but he . . . didn't reply."

BREVITAS. Rapid discussion.

BREVITY. Succinctness of expression. See *ellipsis*.

CACOSINTHETON. *Anastrophe* misused, as in an artificial poetic diction.

CATEGORY. A class or distinction, a differentiation between divisions. See *definition*.

CAUSE. A necessary cause is required to produce the effect; a sufficient cause or precipitating cause might possibly have produced the effect; the immediate cause is that which is closest to the effect produced; the remote cause is that which is farthest removed from the effect. See *etiologia*.

CHARIENTISMUS. Light *banter* that is meant to soothe rancor; for instance, in trying to avoid a fight with a bully one might say, "I'm sure you're too much of a gentleman to want to pick a fight with a coward wearing glasses."

CHIASMUS. A technique of parallel structure, cross-parallelism: "*I vied with the wind*, she fought the air, and as she lost, *I was victorious*." Note that in the first half of this sentence "I" is first, "she" is second, but in the second half of the sentence "she" and "I" are reversed.

CHRONICLE. A chronological record in verse or in prose of events purported to have happened over a long period of time. See also *journalism*.

CIRCUITO. A roundabout argument or manner of speaking. See *circumlocution* and *periphrasis*.

CIRCULATION. The distribution of a periodical. See *journalism*.

CIRCUMLOCUTION. Round-about manner of speaking. See *periphrasis* and *enigma*.

CITY DESK. The province of the city or local editor of a newspaper. See *editor* and *journalism*.

CITY EDITOR. The editor whose responsibility is the local metropolitan area. See *editor* and *journalism*.

CLASSICAL DISCOURSE. Structured as described in detail in the introductory essay of this chapter; the following is a simplified recapitulation:

I. The subject of the discourse is given in the title or in a subtitle.

II. Second, the thesis is introduced.
   A. In the first paragraph the exordium is the statement of the subject being examined and an introduction to the author's argument.
   B. The thesis sentence differs from the subject in that it is a complete statement, usually given in one independent clause or sentence: "In the essay below the proposition *that higher education isn't changing fast enough to keep up with society* is going to be examined and attacked."

III. The third part of the classical discourse is the *argument* itself. This portion of the essay is in three parts:
   A. The *narratio,* or narration, is the exposition of necessary background information concerning subject and thesis.
   B. The *confirmatio,* or confirmation, is the list of arguments, proofs, and facts backing the thesis. It is usually arranged in the order of weakest argument to strongest (auxetic or climactic).
   C. The *refutatio,* or refutation is the rebuttal of all possible arguments to the contrary. It is usually arranged in the order of strongest argument to weakest (meiotic or anticlimactic).

IV. The last part of the essay is the *conclusion* in which there is
   A. A *peroratio,* or peroration, an appeal to emotion as well as to logic.
   B. A restatement, or recapitulation, of the proved thesis and the *resolution* of the argument.

CLASSIFIED AD. A short advertisement in a section of the newspaper reserved for such items in various categories, for instance, "personals," "employment opportunities," and "lawn sales." See *journalism*.

COLUMN, COLUMNIST. One of several vertical portions of printed lines positioned on a page beside but separated from one another. A writer of local or syndicated newspaper feature articles columns. See *journalism*.

COMICS, COMIC STRIP. The cartoons section of a newspaper. See *journalism*.

COMMUNICATIONS MEDIUM, MEDIA (pl.). Newspapers, radio, television, Internet (the World Wide Web). See *journalism*.

COMPAR, COMPARISON. The balance of statements, opposites, sentences.

COMPLEXIO, COMPLEXUS. Repetition.

CONCLUSION. Syllogistic summation; see *syllogism* in text.

CONDUPLICATION. Repetition.

CONJUNCTION. A joining of items, as in "One loves to look at water, AND one loves to swim." See *disjunction*.

CONSTRUCTIONAL SCHEMES. Syntactical strategies for building sentences. They include grammatical parallelism (synonymia, synthesis, antithesis, and auxesis), covered elsewhere in these pages; *anacoluthon, anastrophe, cacosintheton, chiasmus, epitheton, hendiadys, hypallage, hysteron proteron, meiosis, parenthesis, parison, syneciosis,* and *zeugma*.

CONTENTION. Opposition in debate.

CONTINUATION. A series of closing statements.

CONTRAST. The comparision of differences; see *antiphrasis*.

CONVERSATION. A discussion between or among people. See *argument*.

CONVERSION. A synonym for repetition.

COPY. Written material.

CORRECTION. Replacing the erroneous with the accurate: "I do not speak of what is 'meat'—that is, of the flesh, of carnal appetite, but of what is MEET or seemly."

CORRESPONDENT. A letter-writing partner. See *foreign correspondent*.

COSMIC IRONY. See *irony*.

CROSS-EXAMINATION. Hostile examination of a witness or treatment of a witness as hostile. The term has been misused for many years to mean merely "Now it's your turn to examine this witness." See *interrogation.*

CUB REPORTER. See *reporter.*

CURSE. See *anathema* and *imprecation.*

DEBATE. See *argument.*

DECLAMATIO, DECLAMATION. See *oration.*

DECORUM. The suitability of a component of a work, such as style or tone, to its specific situation or to the writing as a whole.

DEFINIENDUM. See the following entry.

DEFINITIO, DEFINITION. *Denotation,* giving the meaning of a definiendum or word to be defined, as has just been done. The essential definition is the most fundamental denotation of a term or concept, placing it in a *category* (genus) and distinguishing it from other members of that category, perhaps answering the question *quid sit,* or "What is its **essence**?" A stipulative definition is required when a word has more than one denotation and the writer must differentiate between them to specify what it is that is being discussed. See also *orismus.*

DENOMINATIO. See *metonymy.*

DEVIL'S ADVOCATE, DEVIL'S DISCIPLE. One who takes the opposite viewpoint in an argument just so that both sides of an issue may be discussed. See *antitheton* and *rhetorical fallacies.*

DIAERESIS. The pronunciation of two contiguous vowels in suddenly different ways, as in "c**oo**peration," "n**eo**logism," unlike the diphthong, which is a gliding from one vowel to another within the same syllable, as in "t**oi**l" or "b**ai**t."

DIALECTIC (dialect). Change in the spelling of a word but not its meaning; for instance, "You sweet thang," for thing, or "Let's go foah a walk in the pahk" for "Let's go for a walk in the park."

DIALISIS. Setting up the propositions of an argument when these propositions appear to be a dilemma (divisio), in that they seem to be mutually exclusive. It must be one or the other proposition, but which is it? Perhaps it is neither, or both—dialisis disposes of both propositions without *paradox*: "You say Jack loves

to live, that brother Jules / Lives to love? Then I say both are
fools: / One must be alive to love at any cost— / Then live to
live, love love, or all is lost."

DIATRIBE. See *argument*.

DIDACTICS. Didactic forms are teaching forms. See *abecedarius*,
alphabestiary, *apologue*, *bestiary*, enigma, *epistle*, example, *exemplum*, *fable*, fabliau, *gnome*, *primer*, *riddle*, and *sententia*.

DIGRESSION. See *parecnasis*.

DILEMMA. See *dialisis*.

DISCOURSE. A *conversation*, or at least one side of an argument.

DISJUNCTIO, DISJUNCTION. Disconnection of items, as in "One
loves to look at water BUT one hates to swim." See *conjunction*.

DISSOLUTIO, DISSOLUTION. See *asyndeton*.

DIT. A synonym for "example," a little story or anecdote illustrating a point.

DIVISIO. See dialisis.

DOUBLE ENTENDRE. See *irony*.

DUBIETY, DUBITATIO, DUBITATION. The ploy of feigned hesitation, as
in the example given under *dialisis* if one had said, "Perhaps so,
but on the other hand, perhaps both are fools."

ECHPHONESIS. *Exclamation* or outcry: "Alas! I am undone!"

ECPHRASIS. Unadorned statement or interpretation.

EDITOR. One who revises and corrects written material prior to its
publication. The editor in chief of a periodical is responsible
for the overall operation and implementation of the policies of
a journal, and the *managing editor* is in charge of its daily operation. Various other editors make up the editorial staff, including the *city editor,* who sits at the *city desk* and is responsible for
local news and coverage assignments (or, in Britain, is in charge
of financial and commercial news); the international editor,
who handles overseas news and materials submitted by the
foreign correspondents who are stationed abroad; the sports editor;
the features editor, and the rewrite editor, who handles material phoned in by *stringers* (see *journalism*).

EDITORIAL. See *journalism*.

EDITORIAL STAFF. See *editor* and *journalism*.

EDITOR IN CHIEF. See *editor* and *journalism*.

EITHER/OR FALLACY. See *rhetorical fallacies*.

ELISION. Dropping syllables from words.

ELLIPSIS. A form of *brevity* that leaves words—generally articles, prepositions, or modifiers—out of clauses and phrases, thereby causing sentences to read in a starker manner than normal: "My love was a faded rose," rather than "My darling love was but a faded rose." See *asyndeton*.

ELLIPTICAL SYLLEPSIS. See *syllepsis*.

EMPHASIS. As discussed in the essays above, it is a range of techniques for stressing a word or a phrase, for instance, by repetition ("He was dumb, dumb, dumb"), by using a different typeface ("He was dumb"), by building a series of synonyms ("He was dumb—I mean, he was ignorant, stupid, and otherwise thick"), and so forth.

ENALLAGE. A rare construction in English, it changes the tense, gender, or number of some part of speech: "God is in **her** heaven; all's right with the world."

ENIGMA. See *didactics*.

EPANALEPSIS. The repetition of a word, for clarity or for emphasis, after the intervention of a word, phrase, or clause. "It is the DUTY of every citizen, the **duty**, I say, to vote."

EPANODIS. Like prolepsis, it expands on a general statement, but in addition it repeats terms contained *in* the general statement, for instance, in a prose piece that begins "In the **kitchen** the **dishwasher** is eating the **dishes**. The Inhabitant listens to the current of digestion—porcelain being **ground**, silver wearing thin, the hum and bite of the machine." And it ends several paragraphs later: "It is as though, the Inhabitant reflects, the women are spinning. It is as though, while he waits, they weave bindings among the rooms; as though the strands of tune were elements of a sisterhood of **dishes**, the ladies, the spider in the cabinet, even of the **dishwasher**, done now with its GRINDING, which contributes a new sound—a continuo of satiety—to the gray motet the **kitchen** is singing."

EPENTHIS. Addition of syllables in the center of a word; for example, "disenfigure" for "disfigure."

EPIPHORA. The repetition of end words or end phrases, as in the poem form called the sestina (see *The Book of Forms*).

EPISTLE. A *letter* used for an informative purpose, such as those in Lord Philip Dormer Chesterfield's book of *Letters* to his son born out of wedlock, the younger Philip Dormer Stanhope. The letters purported to be admonitory but in fact were revelatory of Lord Chesterfield's own lack of character.

EPIMONE. The use of repeated phrases, clauses, or lines at intervals in writing.

EPITHETON. An inserted, synonymous modification of a sentence element, such as a subject: "John Jones, my good friend, is a poet." See also discussion of epithet in text.

EPITROPIS. Used when the speaker believes he has said enough and refers the reader to something else in order to complete the thought: "I've said enough. Time for another martini. You take these definitions on from here."

EPIZEUXIS. Repetition of words without any pause between them: "**Beat, beat, beat,** o drums!"

EQUIVOCATION. See *rhetorical fallacies*.

EROTEMA. The rhetorical question, a question for which no answer is given or expected because, in context, the answer is obvious: "Am I my brother's keeper?" The understood biblical answer is "Yes."

ESSAY. See *magazine*.

ESSENTIAL DEFINITION. See *definition*.

ETIOLOGIA. The argumentative technique of assigning a *cause* or reason for an action or circumstance: "I wish to speak of worms on Mars because no one has done so before."

EUPHEMISM. See *periphrasis*.

EXAMPLE. See exemplum.

EX CATHEDRA. See *rhetorical fallacies*.

EXCLAMATIO, EXCLAMATION. A cry of protest. See also *echphonesis*.

EXCLUSIVE SCHEMES. Strategies for building sentences by leaving things out of them. See *asyndeton*, *aposiopesis*, *ellipsis*, and *syllepsis*.

EXEMPLUM. A parable or *fable*, perhaps—a brief story told to make a moral point, often in a *sermon* or a homily.

EXPEDIENCE, EXPEDITIO, EXPEDITION. Doing whatever is necessary to move the argument forward, including leaving unimportant things out.

EXPLICATION. A synonym for exposition; an explanation, discussed in the lead essay of this chapter.

EXPOSÉ. See *journalism*.

FABLE (or *apologue*). A didactic *allegory* in which the adventures of an animal teach a moral lesson.

FAULTY CAUSE. See *rhetorical fallacies*.

FAULTY HIDDEN GENERALIZATION. See *generalization* and *rhetorical fallacies*.

FEATURE, FEATURES EDITOR. See *editor* and *journalism*.

FEATURES JOURNALISM. See *magazine journalism*.

FIGURAE VERBORUM, FIGURES OF SPEECH. See *rhetorical tropes*.

FLYTING. A formal *harangue* or rant (*invective*, *diatribe*), a debate between poets that can become bitter. See also *The Book of Forms*.

FOREIGN CORRESPONDENT. A reporter who is stationed abroad. See *journalism*.

FRANKNESS. Candor, *parrhesia,* speaking freely.

GENERALIZATION. A statement so broad as to be meaningless: "Poor people deserve to be poor, for they are born lazy." See *rhetorical fallacies*.

GENUS. See *definition*.

GNOME. An *apothegm* or truism, sometimes in rhyming form. Some "gnomic verses" may be found in *The Book of Forms* under the heading of *englyn cyrch*.

GOFER. See *reporter*.

GRADATIO, GRADATION. See *repetition*.

HARANGUE. A diatribe, a furious attack on someone or something; *invective* or *rant*.

HENDIADYS. A construction that treats a double subject or object as though it were singular, not plural, in order to express a thought that is operating on more than one level: "My lust and her adamance is Hell."

HOMILY. See *didactics*.

HOMOGRAPH, HOMOMORPH. A word that is spelled like another word with a totally different meaning, such as bore: "to drill" and bore: "a dull person."

HORIZONTAL AUDIENCE. See *audience*.

HOUSE ORGAN. See *magazine*.

HUMAN INTEREST STORY. See *journalism*.

HYPALLAGE. An exchange of words in phrases or clauses. The technique is used in the first two lines of E. E. Cummings's poem "Anyone Lived in a Pretty How Town": "anyone lived in a pretty how town / with up so floating many bells down."

HYPERBATON. A term that covers the various kinds of dislocation or inversion of grammatic syntax, including *anastrophe, cacosinthe-ton,* and *hypallage*.

HYPERBOLE (or *superlatio*). Calculated exaggeration, overstatement: "Her eyes were as large as two cratered moons"; the opposite of *litotes,* which is studied understatement.

HYPERRHYTHM. See *diaeresis*.

HYPHAERESIS. A technique of overt elision that drops a consonant rather than a vowel from the center of a word in order to telescope two syllables and make them one, as in "whene'er" for **whenever**.

HYPOZEUGMA. See zeugma.

HYPOZEUXIS. The repetition of words in parallel constructions. The repeated words govern the sense of the clause or clauses of which they are a part: "Up to **the door** I'll go, and at **the door** I'll rap."

HYSTERON PROTERON. The reversal of chronological events for purposes of intensification or stress: "Let us break our necks and jump" rather than "Let us jump and break our necks."

ILLUSTRATION. See *magazine*.

IMMEDIATE CAUSE. See *cause*.

IMPLIED APOSIOPESIS. Substituting another letter, syllable, word, or passage for the dropped material: "You are an as**phyxiating** person." See *aposiopesis*.

IMPRECATION. Curse. See *anathema*.

INCLUSIVE SCHEMES. Strategies for building sentences by including items. See *enallage, irmus, merismus,* and *prolepsis*.

INSERTS. See *journalism*.

INSUFFICIENT SAMPLING. Sampling that provides insufficient data from too small a pool of specimens; *unrepresentative*.

INTELLECTIO. See *synechdoche*.

INTERLOCUTOR. One who questions. See *irony* and *interrogatory*.

INTERNATIONAL EDITOR. See *editor* and *journalism*.

INTERPRETATIO, INTERPRETATION. See *reiteration*.

INTERROGATIO, INTERROGATORY. A summary challenge, as in *cross-examination*.

INVECTIVE. Language that is abusive or vituperative, as in the *curse*, an execration or profane utterance; in profanity, irreverent language, or in desecration, a violation of the sacred, sacrilege. See *argument*.

INVESTIGATIVE REPORTING. See *journalism*.

IPSE DIXIT. See *rhetorical fallacies*.

IRMUS. Suspended sense. Not until the end of a passage does the reader fully understand what is being spoken of: "Soft as goosedown, smooth as velvet, round as a bowl, as full of love as it is of satisfaction, is my kitten's **belly**."

IRONIA. See *irony*.

IRONICAL ALLUSION. Also called *allegorical allusion* or permutation: "Ah, beware the **didies** [instead of the **ides**] of March"— "didies," of course, being diapers or nappies.

IRONY. Witty mockery, usually effected by saying the opposite of what is actually meant: "I'd love to go with you into the tar pit, but unfortunately I find myself involved in a rather sticky situation of my own." Socratic irony is the feigning of ignorance and a willingness to be enlightened by an *interlocutor*, a teacher or questioner.

Double entendre is speaking with a twofold meaning, one of which—the secondary or implied meaning—is generally off-color or salacious. An entire work that sustains a double meaning is said to contain structural irony, as in the allegory in the chapter on "The Genres of Fiction"; see also *didactics*. *Cosmic irony* has to do with the gods toying with human beings, teasing and tormenting and then destroying them perhaps, as though they were of no consequence.

Romantic irony is a form of *metaliterature*, in which the narrator from time to time commits what has elsewhere been called *authorial intrusion* by taking the reader into her or his confidence and pointing out that the fiction is really nothing but verbal manipulation, not real life. See also *metafiction*, *metadrama*, metapoetry (in text; see also *The Book of Forms*), *paradiastole*.

JEREMIAD. A speech or writing prophesying doom or a lamentation filled with bitterness. See *philippic*.

JEST. A joke. See *asteismus*.

JEU D'ESPRIT. A synonym for *bagatelle*, a clever or witty piece of humor.

JOURNALISM. *Chronicles* published on a daily, weekly, or monthly basis are newspaper journalism: a record of the events of the day, as displayed in *news items*, or reports of daily occurrences on the local, area, national, and international scenes, including sports and weather; *news of record*, including births, deaths, *obituaries*, property sales, and tax *notices*; political material, including voting information; *columns* (written by *columnists*) expressing the *obiter dicta* or passing views of the writer who may be either a local columnist or a syndicated columnist whose work appears in several newspapers simultaneously; editorials, or comments appearing on the *op-ed* [opposite editorial] page by the *editors* and *publisher* of the publication on news of interest; *letters to the editor*; features, including everything from human interest material to *comic strips*, women's pages, and even fiction and poetry in inserts such as Sunday supplements. Most newspapers are supported by *advertising*, including *classified* and *personal* ads, and advertisers are interested in the *circulation* of the journal, including *newsstand* sales but particularly subscription sales.

There are various types of journalism. *Yellow journalism* is sensational reporting or *scandalmongering*, in such papers as *scandal sheets* and *tabloids*. A *muckraker* is one who searches out misfeasance, malfeasance, and corruption among public officials using the techniques of investigative journalism and writes about them in the exposé. A *slant* is a subtly biased news article; an *angle* is an unusual viewpoint, a "peg" on which to hang a story that will be different from the treatment given it by any other public *communications medium* (plural, *media*).

Print journalism is the oldest of the media, which now include radio and television journalism, and the "communications highway" Internet (web) of the modem-equipped *pc* (personal computer).

LATINITAS. Correctness or accuracy.

LETTER. A written message sent to a correspondent; an *epistle*. See *didactics*.

LETTERS TO THE EDITOR. Communications sent by readers to the editor of a periodical, responding to something printed in that journal. See *journalism*.

LITOTES. Deliberate understatement, for instance, "Adolf Hitler was a naughty man."

LITTLE MAGAZINE. A literary periodical with a limited circulation. See *magazine*.

LOGICAL FALLACY. A failure in reasoning, or an incorrect argument. See *rhetorical fallacies*.

MAGAZINE, MAGAZINE JOURNALISM. Features journalism, often intended for specific audiences: women, sports enthusiasts, hobbies, collecting, and so forth. A magazine is therefore a collection of articles, essays, features, *illustrations* (artwork) and photographs appealing to a segment of the reading public. The staffs of such periodicals will be similar to those of *newspapers*, although there will generally not be such a wide range of editorships, except, of course, in *newsmagazines*. There are many types of magazines, ranging from trade journals, which appeal to plumbers, carpenters, electricians, and so forth, through house organs, which are *newsletters* distributed to the employees of a particular industry, organization, business, or corporation; to academic or scientific quarterlies, and *little magazines* which publish poetry, fiction, nonfiction, and other creative materials for very limited audiences.

MALEDICTION. Calling upon the gods to visit evil upon someone; also a slander. See *anathema*, *curse*, and *imprecation*.

MANAGING EDITOR. The editor of a journal who is in charge of daily operations. See *editor* and *journalism*.

MASS CIRCULATION. Large-scale distribution of a journal. See *audience* and *circulation*.

MATERIAL FALLACIES. See *rhetorical fallacies*.

MAXIM. An *adage* or wise saying. See *didactics*.

MEDIA. Shorthand for "communications media"; the Latin plural for medium, meaning "method" or "means." See *journalism*.

MEDIUM. See preceding entry.

MEIOSIS. *Anticlimax*—ending at the weakest point, the nadir, rather than at the strongest point, the apex.

MEMBER, MEMBRUM. An identifiable part of the whole, for instance, a clause or a phrase in a sentence.

MERISMUS. Expanding on a subject by particularizing each element of it.

MESOZEUGMA. See zeugma.

METALEPSIS. Substitution for a word of a synonym that is essentially metaphorical, in that the equation between the word and its synonym is not obvious. For instance, at one time a sailor's trousers had a front flap that was secured with thirteen buttons, and one might have said, "I met Ray just as he first thumbed the last of thirteen buttons," instead of "I met Ray on the day he enlisted in the navy."

METALITERATURE. Literature about literature. See *irony*; also see other chapters and *The Book of Forms* for *metafiction*, *metadrama*, and *metapoetry*, and see the opening essay of this chapter for *metanonfiction*.

METANOIA. Making a statement and then retracting it by substituting something else: "They tell me that your head is filled with rocks. I don't believe it . . . but maybe solid bone."

METANONFICTION. Nonfiction about nonfiction. See *metaliterature* and the opening essay of this chapter.

METASTASIS. The technique of flitting from one argument to another quickly, much as a boxer bobs and weaves so that his opponent can't get a good shot at him.

METATHESIS. Transposition of the letters of a word, as in the *anagram*, which is a word, phrase, or sentence constructed by rearranging the letters of another word, phrase, or sentence: "live" = "vile," "stunted" = "student."

METONYMY (or denominatio). A way of describing by using a word related to a word rather than the original word itself: "The HEART will find a way" rather than "Love will find a way."

MICTERISMUS. Verbal sneering, as in "The old professor knows that books are safe. He knows he's really Samson on the make, too smart to lose his hair."

MORGUE. The clippings library of a newspaper.

MORGUE CLERK. The person in charge of a newspaper "morgue." See *reporter*.

MUCKRAKER. A reporter concerned with *muckraking*.

MUCKRAKING. Journalism concerned with digging up political scandal and public corruption. See *journalism*.

NAME-CALLING. Slander. See *rhetorical fallacies*.

NECESSARY CAUSE. See *cause*.

NEWS ITEM. An article in a journal. See *journalism*.

NEWSLETTER. The journal of an organization or business of some kind. See *magazine*.

NEWSMAGAZINE. A newspaper in magazine format. See *magazine*.

NEWS OF RECORD. News items having to do with births, deaths, tax information, public meetings, and so forth. See *journalism*.

NEWSMAN, NEWSPERSON, NEWSWOMAN. See *reporter*.

NEWSPAPER, NEWSPAPER JOURNALISM. See *journalism*.

NEWSSTAND. A kiosk or store that sells newspapers. See *journalism*.

NOEMA. An ironic way (see *irony*) of speaking by saying one thing on the surface but meaning something quite different: "You say Fred lives his life without a taint? You're right. I wish to God he were a saint"—meaning, on the surface level, that the speaker agrees with the appraisal of Fred but meaning in fact that the speaker wishes Fred were dead, as only the dead can be saints.

NONMETAPHORIC FIGURES. Figures of speech other than descriptions, similes, and metaphors. See *rhetorical tropes*.

NON SEQUITUR. An argument that does not proceed from its premise. See *rhetorical fallacies*.

NOTICES. News of record regarding public deadlines and meetings. See *journalism*.

OBITER DICTA. Personal opinions or remarks. See *journalism*.

OBITUARY. A death notice. See *journalism*.

OBJECTIVE REPORTING, OBJECTIVITY. The ability to observe and report situations without bias. See *rhetorical fallacies*.

OP-ED. "Opposite editorial." See *journalism*, *obiter dicta*.

ORATION. A speech delivered in a formal manner, a declamation.

ORISMUS. A *definition* that is different from someone else's definition of a word or phrase: "The school's a madhouse? I doubt it, but a group therapy program, maybe."

ORTHOGRAPHICAL SCHEMES. Having to do with the forms of words and syllables, with spelling. See *schemes* and *orthography*. Orthographical schemes include amphisbaenia, anagram, antisthecon, aphaeresis, apocope, diaeresis, dialectic, homograph, homonym, epenthis, hyphaeresis, metathesis, palindrome, proparalepsis, prosthesis, syncope, synalepha, and tmesis.

ORTHOGRAPHY. Correct spelling.

OVERT ELISION. Skipping a syllable, as in "do**n't**." See *elision*.

PALINDROME. A word, phrase, clause, or larger unit that reads the same backward as forward (e.g., "radar"; "Able was I ere I saw Elba."

PARADIASTOLE. Use of an *antonym* rather than a *synonym* to ironic effect (see *irony*); for instance, if one were speaking of a cheapskate, one might say, "Skinflint is **generous** to a fault" or, of a coward, "He **bravely** rose in battle and ran away."

PARADOX. A metaphor or statement that combines terms that seem mutually exclusive but in fact are not: "Freedom is the prison of rebellion," or "Winter is the Spring of contemplation." Also, a statement that contradicts a commonly held belief: "The earth is not round, it is egg-shaped." See also *dialisis*.

PARAGOGE. Adding a sound or sounds to the end of a word, as in "Ros**ie**" for **Rose** or "bought**en**" for **bought**.

PARAGON. The argumentative technique of quickly summing up and rejecting all reasons for making a particular point except the one reason the arguer believes to be valid.

PARALEPSIS. Making a little thing of something by passing over it lightly or denying its importance and thereby emphasizing its actual importance through understatement: "Well, here's our all-American boy. What's there to say of him? He has a pretty wife, and he keeps his hair neatly cut."

PARAMALOGIA. Admission of arguments to the contrary so as to undercut the opponent's case, as in the example for *noema*.

PARAPHRASE. Repeating something in different words. See *reiteration*. See also synonymous parallelism in text.

PARECNASIS. The technique of digression—leaving one's main argument for a time to talk of other things, which, for the moment, may not seem pertinent but which in fact bolster the main point when one returns to it.

PARENTHESIS. The insertion of material that interrupts the thought: "I was going—or have I told you this?—to go away").

PARIMIA. The trope of speaking by means of *proverbs*: "'An apple a day keeps the doctor away.' That's no doubt true, for he expects to be paid with money."

PARISIA. An *apologia* (i.e., an apology) or explanation by the writer of scurrilous or licentious material that justifies his or her having done so: "Forgive me for being somewhat off-color, but you know what it's like when you're being osculated." Or the apology may be for one's life, as in the case of Cardinal New-man, who wrote an *Apologia pro Vita Sua*; or for anything else, such as the *Apologie for Poetry* by Philip Sidney (1554–1586). A poem form of the apology is the palinode; see *The Book of Forms*.

PARISON. Sentence construction by parallel clauses of equal weight, as in Caesar's statement, "I came, I saw, I conquered."

PARONOMASIA. A synonym for *annomination*.

PARRHESIA. Frankness, the opposite of *periphrasis*.

PARTICULA PENDENS. See *anacoluthon*.

PC. Personal computer. If it is capitalized, PC, it means "politically correct." (It may also mean "Professional Corporation," which would be, at a minimum, a "pair o' dox.") See also *journalism*.

PERIPHRASIS. Beating about the bush. Saying something in words other than those that are most to the point. It is often a way of saying something in a more grandiloquent or roundabout way than is usual ("She was taken unto the bosom of her forebears," rather than "She died"). A euphemism is a nicer word or phrase substituted for another that is likely to offend; its opposite is *parrhesia*, which is *frankness*. See *didactics*.

PERMISSION. Yielding: "Ah, yes, without a doubt I think you're right. It's better to love one's sweetheart than to fight." A synonym is concession.

PERMUTATION. See *ironical allusion*.

PERSONAL AD. An advertisement placed by an individual or group in the "personals" column of the classified ads section of a journal. See *journalism*.

PERSONIFICATION. Treating an inanimate object or an abstraction as though it were a human being: "As the airplane climbed, the cloud enveloped us as though it were a lover."

PHILIPPIC. A vicious written or spoken indictment of something or someone.

PHOTOJOURNALISM. News reporting in which photography is the primary carrier of the news, with written *copy* merely supplementing the visual material. See *journalism*.

PLOCE. The repetition of words or phrases at irregular intervals.

POLEMICS. Debating techniques such as are to be found in *classical discourse* and in other types of *argument*. See *rhetorical tropes*.

POLYPTOTON. The repetition of words derived from the same root: "He **ran**, will **run**, and is **running** now."

POLYSYNDETON. The repetition of conjunctions, the opposite of *asyndeton*, and to be distinguished from *anaphora*.

POST HOC ERGO PROPTER HOC. "After this, therefore because of this." See *rhetorical fallacies*.

PRÆCISIO. An uncompleted sentence.

PRÆTERITIO, PRETERITION. The act of passing over fleetly: "Healing is what is important (though of course there was a wound), and we must focus on getting well rather than upon incidental matters."

PRECIPITATING CAUSE. See *cause*.

PRESSMAN. In Britain pressman is a synonym for *reporter*, but in the United States and elsewhere it means the operator of the printing presses of a newspaper.

PRIMER. A book used to teach the alphabet, often written in primer couplet as in *The New England Primer*. See also *abecedarius* and *didactics*.

PRINT JOURNALISM. News publication that uses the printing press. See *journalism*.

PROCATALEPSIS. Preempting opposing arguments by anticipating the argument before the opponent can articulate it: "Oh, yes, it's true; the world's a sack of worms, but if we're robins we can come to terms."

PROLEPSIS. Expansion on a general statement, particularizing it and giving further information regarding it.

PRONOMINATION. A synonym for *antonomasia*.

PROPARALEPSIS. Addition of syllables at the end of a word (i.e., "figur**ation**" for "figure").

PROPORTION. Pleasing or sufficient relationships of the elements constituting a whole; symmetry and balance, as in parallel construction.

PROSONOMASIA. A way of nicknaming someone by substituting a letter or letters in that person's name to describe him or her by some personal characteristic; for instance, if a very thin person were named "Jones," one might substitute a **B** for the **J** and call her or him **B**ones.

PROTHESIS. Added syllables at the beginning of a word (i.e., "**con**-figuration" for figuration, both of which mean figure or image, or as in "The cock's on the midden **a**-blowing his horn").

PROVERB. A wise traditional saying; see *adage*, *didactics*, and *parimia*.

PROZEUGMA. See zeugma.

PSYCHOLOGICAL FALLACIES. See *rhetorical fallacies*.

PUBLISHER. The publisher is the owner of a book publishing concern or of a *periodical*, or the agent of the owner, whose responsibility it is to oversee its publication. See *journalism*.

PUN. A joke that relies on ambiguity and irony: "When did your sands of Yuma desert you?" See *annomination*.

QUARTERLY. See *magazine*.

QUID SIT. See *definition*.

RANT. See *argument*.

RATIOCINATIO, RATIOCINATION. Self-questioning: "If I were a fleeing criminal, where would I go?"

REASON. See *etiologia*.

RED HERRING. See *rhetorical fallacies*.

REDUCTIO AD ABSURDUM. See *rhetorical fallacies*.

REITERATION, REPETITIO, REPETITION. The word "repetition" itself denotes initial repetition, for instance, "**Who** am I, **who** are you, and **who** shall we be together?" Gradatio or gradation is linking repetition: "Who am **I**? **I** am he who comes to see you." *Conversio, conversion* is end repetition, as is required in the verse form called the sestina (see in *The Book of Forms*), and *complexio* or *complexus* is the combination of repetition and conversion.

Traductio, traduction (**not** traducement), expolitio, and commoratio are iteration (and reiteration), as is conduplicatio (*conduplication*), but interpretatio (interpretation) is iteration by *paraphrase*. See *synonymous parallelism* in text.

REMOTE CAUSE. See *cause*.

REPETITIONAL SCHEMES. Strategies for building sentences that contain repeated elements. See *anadiplosis, anaphora, antanaclasis, antimetabole, antistrophe, emphasis, epanalepsis, epanodis, epimone, epizeuxis, hypozeuxis, ploce, polyptoton, reiteration,* and *symploce*.

REPORTER, REPORTING. Reporters and *stringers* (freelance or part-time reporters) who are in the field covering *beats*, such as the police beat, and stories. A cub reporter is an apprentice *newsperson* who sometimes acts as a gofer (messenger or menial) and perhaps doubles as a *morgue clerk,* or clipping files librarian.

RETRACTION. See *metanoia*.

REWRITE EDITOR. See *editor* and *journalism*.

RHETORICAL FALLACIES. *Logical fallacies* are those that stem from faulty reasoning; material fallacies are errors caused by flaws in the subject matter; psychological fallacies appeal to the biases and emotions of the audience. Argumentative fallacies include the *ad hominem*, which attempts to transfer the burden of the argument away from the issue in question to an attack on the person opposing the speaker or writer: "It's all very well for Newt Gingrich to espouse 'family values,' but wasn't he raised by a single mother? Didn't he divorce his wife when she became ill? And why does he deplore the Lesbian life style—is it not his sister's?" In the appeal to authority (a church authority proclaiming a doctrine does so *ex cathedra*, "from the pulpit"), the essayist cites a person with an impressive reputation in the field; *ipse dixit* is a forceful assertion that an authority has said a particular thing and that it is therefore so, without offering proof. The appeal to force threatens the audience with dire consequences. The appeal to humor is a diversionary tactic that directs the attention away from the question in hand. The appeal to ignorance avers that the argument must be true because the opponent cannot prove it is false. The appeal to pity attempts to enlist the sympathy of the audience at the expense of reason: "Yes, it is true that this young woman at the age of fourteen bludgeoned her mother to death with a hammer, but though she is still young, she has paid her debt to society and deserves an education. Why did Harvard revoke her application when it discovered she had committed matricide?"

The appeal to tradition plays to conservative feelings. The bandwagon fallacy is the argument that the audience ought to do as others have done. The either/or fallacy is a reductio ad absurdum, reducing a complicated thesis to only two choices: "Either all women are feeling creatures, or they are not. If they are not, they are not women." Equivocation utilizes the same term in two different ways: "Walter is the lover of Jennifer, but Jennifer is a lover of clothes."

The faulty cause is the *post hoc ergo propter hoc* fallacy—"after this, therefore because of this": "In the twelve years since Mario Cuomo took office as governor of New York State the ability of students to read has plummeted throughout the nation." The faulty hidden generalization has a false missing premise in the enthymeme: "He displays the American flag, so he must be patriotic."

Name-calling uses cues and stereotypes to impugn an opponent. A non sequitur is a *conclusion* that does not follow from the premise or proposition on which an *argument* is based, as in the catachretic syllogism discussed above. The red herring is a deliberate and irrelevant distraction from the true subject or argument. The rigged question is a a verbal trap that requires a conclusion of guilt no matter how it is answered: "Do you beat your wife, or do you merely abuse her by shouting at her?" A straw man is a setup, something erected so as to be easily destroyed, such as an argument so preposterous as to be refuted seemingly without effort: "My opponent believes that all people are created equal, which is an easy thing for a person born into wealth to argue. What about those of us who are born into poverty?"

RHETORICAL QUESTION. See *erotema*.

RHETORICAL TROPES. Certain *figures of speech* may be called rhetorical tropes (*figurae verborum*) because they are concerned with making their effects through *nonmetaphoric figures of speech*.

RIDDLE. The riddle, or enigma, is a guessing game in which the *ambage,* or ambiguous *circumlocution* (roundabout manner of speaking; see *periphrasis*) is used. See *didactics.* For examples, see *The Book of Forms.*

RIGGED QUESTION. See *rhetorical fallacies.*

ROMANTIC IRONY. See *irony.*

SCANDALMONGERING, SCANDAL SHEETS. "Yellow" journalism. See *journalism* and *rhetorical fallacies.*

SCHEMAS, SCHEMES. Strategies that have to do with changes in normal syntax, in word order, or in parts of words. There are several types. *Constructional schemes* have to do with the construction of balanced sentences (look elsewhere in these pages under grammatical parallelism). *Exclusive schemes* are strategies for leaving things out of sentences, whereas *inclusive schemes* insert words or other elements. *Orthographical schemes* change, add, or delete syllables in particular words. *Substitutive schemes* exchange sentence elements, and *repetitional schemes* reiterate them.

SEGUE. See *transition.*

SELECTIVE CITATION. The citing of materials in such a way as to support one's own argument while avoiding details that would tend to undercut it. See *rhetorical fallacies.*

SENTENTIA. Common or received wisdom, often in the form of maxims or "old saws," sometimes rhymed; *adages, aphorisms, axioms, proverbs,* or truisms.

SERMON, SERMONICATIO. Direct *discourse.*

SETUP. See *rhetorical fallacies.*

SIMILITUDE, SIMILITUDO. Similarity of two or more objects. See *comparison.*

SLANT. The *bias* of the conductor of an argument; see *journalism* and *rhetorical fallacies.*

SOCRATIC IRONY. See *irony.*

SPEECH. See *argument.*

SPOONERISM. Transposition of the initial sounds of two words in a clause, as in one of the most famous slips of the tongue of the Rev. William Archibald Spooner (1844–1930): "Young man, you've **t**asted the whole **w**orm!" (instead of "you've **w**asted the whole **t**erm!").

SPORTS EDITOR. See *editor* and *journalism.*

STASIS. The technique of dwelling at length on one's strongest argument.

STEREOTYPE. A superficial characterization: "My opponent has never had to work a day in his life. What does he know about the laborer's situation?"

STIPULATIVE DEFINITION. See *definition.*

STRAW MAN. See *rhetorical fallacies.*

STRINGER. A part-time reporter. See *editor* and *reporter.*

STRUCTURAL IRONY. See *irony.*

SUBSCRIPTION. See *journalism.*

SUBSTITUTION. See *metanoia* and *substitutive schemes.*

SUBSTITUTIVE SCHEMES. Replacement of sentence elements with other, dissimilar elements. See *anaphora, antanaclasis, anthimeria, antonomasia, hyperbole, implied aposiopesis, litotes, metalepsis, metonymy, paradiastole, periphrasis, prosonomasia,* and *synechdoche.*

SUFFICIENT CAUSE. See *cause.*

SUMMARY. See *continuation.*

SUNDAY SUPPLEMENT, SUPPLEMENT. See *journalism.*

SUPERLATIO. See *hyperbole.*

SYLLEPSIS. There are two kinds: (1) a grammatical construction in which one part of speech controls two other elements, agreeing with only one of them ("She kisses me, and I [kiss] her"); and (2) zeugmatic, which has a part of speech correctly controlling two other elements but controlling them in different ways ("He waited with mind and dagger sharp").

SYMPLOCE. A combination of *anaphora* **or** *antistrophe* and *epiphora.*

SYNALEPHA. A technique of overt elision by means of which one of two adjacent unaccented vowels is suppressed in order to achieve the effect of only one unaccented syllable, as in "th' art of poetic diction."

SYNCOPE. A technique of overt elision that drops a syllable from the center of a word: "suff'ring" for **suffering**.

SYNECDOCHE (or intellectio). Substituting a part for the whole, as in "He was the king's **legs**" rather than "He was the king's messenger."

SYNECIOSIS. Cross–coupling antonyms in such a way as to make them agree: "We are ourselves **victim** and **victor**. In killing you we murder an emblem of what we strive to be: not men, but Man."

SYNONYM. A word of similar meaning; for instance, **creep** is a synonym for **crawl**, and **fly** is a synonym for **soar**. See *constructional schemes*. See also synonymous parallelism in text.

TABLOID. A reference not only to the smaller size of a newspaper but to the kind of sensational journalism published in such periodicals. See *journalism*.

TACT. The suitability of the approach of an argument to the sensibility of the reader or audience.

TAPINOSIS. Saying too little of a subject; undersaying, **not** *litotes*, which is understatement, nor *anticlimax*.

TASIS. Musicality in language.

TMESIS. The breaking up of a compound word, usually by insertion of a related word, as in "**When** you **ever** go" instead of "whenever you go."

TRADE MAGAZINE. See *magazine*.

TRADUCTIO, TRADUCTION. See *repetition*.

TRANSGRESSIO, TRANSGRESSION. See *hyperbaton*.

TRANSITIO, TRANSITION. The passage from one topic to another, segue.

TRUISM. See *didactics*.

UNDERSAYING. See *tapinosis*.

UNDERSTATEMENT. See *litotes*.

UNREPRESENTATIVE SAMPLING. See *insufficient sampling*.

VERTICAL AUDIENCE. See *audience*.

WORDPLAY. See *annomination*.

YELLOW JOURNALISM. Reportage that specializes in the sensational and the scandalous. See *journalism*.

ZEUGMA. To be distinguished from zeugmatic syllepsis, a yoking or binding together of two sentence elements by means of another element, which would otherwise have had to be repeated elsewhere in the sentence. Three kinds of zeugma have been distinguished: prozeugma, in which the binding element precedes the parts it binds ("Everyone wishes to come, and [everyone] will do so, regardless"); mesozeugma, in which the binding element is between the yoked parts ("This is the place he loved, and the woman [he loved]"); and hypozeugma, in which the binding element follows the yoked parts ("Neither life [need be feared], nor death itself need be feared").

ZEUGMATIC SYLLEPSIS. See *syllepsis*.

The Genres of Literary Criticism and Scholarship

Criticism is the *written analysis* and *evaluation* of works of art, in-cluding the *artifices* of literature; and all criticism operates on the level of *convention*, a mode of procedure mutually agreeable to members of a society—specifically, to a writer and his or her audi-ence. In the case of poetry, for example, inasmuch as all *prosodies* are basically arbitrary, *verse writing* would be impossible without conventions. Revolutionary change in literature is usually, if not always, caused by the attempts of a writer or group of writers to impose new conventions on an audience, and one of the major purposes of criticism is to explain these changes to the audience, which may or may not accept them. Often it is a *seminal* work of great originality and influence that changes the course of literary development, such as the compendious *Anatomy of Melancholy* of Robert Burton (1577–1640), which gathered together all the known literature and information on the subject that moderns call depression and was therefore, in effect, the first psychological trea-tise in English at the same time that it was an insight into the daily life and the mental condition of Renaissance Britain. It is in this sense that Burton used the word *anatomy*, which means "dissec-tion," for he conducted a forensic dissection of the subject of mel-ancholy in his book.

Seminal critical works in the field of poetry are very often the product of the poets themselves. An *agonist* is a poet, like Coleridge or Wallace Stevens, who spends a great deal of time proselytizing for a particular *theory* of poetry. The *amateur poet* also proselytizes for a viewpoint, but it usually has nothing to do with theories of poetry; rather, like the American poets Denise Levertov and Adrienne Rich, for example, the poetry that amateurs write generally supports a social cause of some sort: antiwar, Ban the Bomb, Save the Whales. A critic who believes that poetry has value for such extrinsic reasons is called a *Platonic critic*. The *professional poet* is one who simply devotes a lifetime to the practice of poetry, *language art;* and a critic who believes that poetry has value for such intrinsic reasons may be thought of as an *Aristotelian critic*. The terms "amateur" and "professional," in this sense, have nothing to do with the ability of a writer to make a living at writing, nor do they raise issues of quality, for both amateur and professional poets are capable of writing poor poetry or good. An *exemplar* is that practicing poet whose work represents the embodiment of a poetic theory, as Walt Whitman's work represents the transcendental/romantic theory of Ralph Waldo Emerson.

Criticism has always depended on the *climate of opinion* that prevails in a particular culture during a specific historical period—the *ambience* (or *ambiance*), the prevailing mood of the *literati* who are concerned with criticism. Thus, in the Romantic period in England, despite the fact that the American colonies had not long before broken away from the empire and this revolution had inspired the French Revolution, many members of the British literary *intelligentsia* were at first inclined to support Napoleon Bonaparte. The climate of opinion in *intellectual circles* supported revolutionary ideas and created the *milieu* in which *Romanticism* could flourish. The *ethos* of a period has to do with its moral tone and ethical values; a synonym is *zeitgeist*. The ethos of a time or society may or may not be in conformity with the climate of opinion.

Textual criticism includes such disciplines as *research; collation* (comparison of texts, editions, printings, or versions); and *exegesis* or *close reading,* of a text (*contextualism,* the French *explication de texte,* or *textual analysis*).

Another type of textual analysis is *hermeneutics,* which is the theory, not the practice, of *interpretation,* particularly of the Bible. There are four types of hermeneutics that have been distinguished traditionally: *literal, allegorical, moral,* and *anagogical.* Two techniques of hermeneutical exegesis are the interlinear or marginal *gloss* (q.v.), or *scholium* (a note in an ancient text), and the *expositio,* a discussion or commentary, either marginal or freestanding. In Bible study a *typos* (type) or *figura* (figure) is an Old Testament character, occurrence, or object that *prefigures* analogous New Testament characters, occurrences, or objects (see *Neoplatonism,* below). A *vulgate* is a generally accepted text of a work; if the Bible, the word begins with a capital letter, *Vulgate.* The uncapitalized term also can mean *vernacular. The higher criticism* is a term signifying the scholarly attempt to isolate such aspects of a biblical text as its author, *provenance* (date, place and proof of origin or derivation), authorial *intention,* and *historicity* (historical authenticity). *Lower criticism* refers to the scholarly attempt to establish an accurate form of the text itself.

Judicial or *evaluative criticism* approaches the text objectively, analyzing it technically and applying to it standards of literary excellence.

Critical Theory

There have been many *critical theories,* both creative and learned, over the centuries. Aristotelian *mimesis* (*mimetic criticism*) is the reproduction in literature and art of the actual world as it is apprehended by the human senses and of human actions in the world. It is the theory that art must be truer to life than life. Mimetic art must induce in the audience what Wordsworth and Coleridge called a "willing suspension of disbelief" (see *convention*) so that the *artifice of form* does not obtrude but rather supports the *illusion* that what occurs in the artifice is a true mirror of nature, or reality (see *unities, imitation*). *Pragmatic* or *practical criticism* views all art as being *affective*—that is, intending to produce in the reader or audience a particular effect or set of effects, and the purpose of this type of criticism is to analyze how the artist, through his or her writing techniques, managed to cause the reader or audience to respond as desired. It is this sort of art, created through *rhetorical tropes*, that Plato disliked but that Aristotle studied. *Rhetorical criticism* is a later simile.

Plato was suspicious of, if not hostile to, the idea of "literature"—first, because *discourse* is the preferred method of learning, for it is interactive, not static, which is perhaps the primary reason that he chose the method of the literary *Socratic dialogue* in which to write his treatises, so as to approximate speech; second, because mimesis is merely an imitation of reality, not reality itself, and it appeals to the emotions primarily, not the intellect.

Aristotle opposed his teacher's view, arguing that mimetic art can and should be profoundly intellectual. He distinguished between forms of drama, insisting that *tragedy* has a high *moral purpose*, not merely an emotive appeal like *comedy*, which displays base or ethically imperfect personalities. Furthermore, of all creatures on earth, mankind is the most imitative, learning nearly everything by mimicry, from which we derive pleasure.

The Roman *odist* and *satirist* Horace (65–8 B.C.) agreed that *dulce et utile* (pleasure and usefulness) were the sole ends of poetry. However, following Plato rather than Aristotle, St. Augustine (354–430) condemned secular literature, in particular poetry and drama, which, being fictive and therefore fabrications, he called *fabula*, fables. For the next millenium, this view of writing was widely held. Nevertheless, Augustine is given credit for founding the science of symbolic signification (*signa*), *semiology*, which would evolve into the twentieth century's *semiotics*.

Augustine believed that one's experience of God, the ultimate reality of existence and the *logos*, the Word made flesh, was bound up with language, which, though an imperfect and ambiguous vehicle, gave mankind at least hints of the will and the nature of the Creator. He discussed both *natural signs* and *conventional signs*; an example of the former (*unintentional signs*) would be footprints in the mud; of the latter (*intentional signs*), words or *hieroglyphics* (pictures representing words, *pictographs*). *Scriptural signs* belonged in the second category, and these were further subdivided into *signa propria*, literal signs, and *signa translata*. The former were to be taken literally, the latter symbolically, needing to be analyzed *hermeneutically*. Likewise *philology*, an understanding of languages (*linguarium notitia*) could be brought to bear upon the former, and science—both social and hard *rerum notitia*—could be utilized to understand the latter.

In his manuscript *De Dialectica,* Augustine held that the ambiguities of language were not the fault of the words themselves but of the various purposes of the users of the words. In *De Trinitate* he likens his *epistemology*—the branch of philosophy that investigates the characteristics of understanding, its elements, assumptions, cogency, and boundaries—to the rhetorical trope *aenigma* (*enigma*), which combines *riddle* and *simile;* for through an investigation of enigmas (*aenigmata*) one may also glean hints and glimmers of the attributes of the Creator. Augustine urged a twofold approach to the theory of signs: *lectio* (reading) and *praedicatio* (preaching), that is, hermeneutics and rhetoric.

The basis of medieval critical theory was *translatio studii*, examining and commenting on literary texts in the light of classical precepts derived from ancient wisdom. Four classes of criticism existed: *Neoplatonism*, which developed from the hermeneutics of the fathers of early Christianity; *Neoaristotelianism*, which derived from principles of logic and scientific analysis; *Horatian*, which rested on a heritage of prosodics and poetics, and *grammatical*, based on classical *stylistics*. The basic method of all these overlapping schools was *enarratio poetarum,* or "exposition of the poets," that is, analysis of and commentary on literary texts and linguistic scrutiny.

The Neoplatonists, including the founder of the school, Plotinus (A.D. 205–70) and his disciple Porphyry believed that the human soul aspired to transcendent experience and that the material world was therefore to be interpreted through poetry that would illuminate the design that underlay apparent chaos. Macrobius (ca. 400) distinguished two types of fictions: pastimes (*social poetry*) and fables (*narratio fabulosa*), which had the serious purpose of illustrating ideas. Even pagan *myth* might thus be examined to discover Christian truths, according to Fulgentius (ca. 500–600) and Boethius (480–524). Neoplatonists also believed in the concept of the "Great Poet," such as the Roman Virgil (70–19 B.C.), whose work had much to recommend it as an illuminator of many sorts of truth. The term *integumentum,* or veil, came to replace fabula in referring to the cloak of fiction that hides the core of truth inherent in myth from the eye of the unsophisticated reader. This word was not a synonym of *allegoria* (allegory), which applies to the several levels of interpretation that may be investigated in the Holy Scriptures. Both terms would bolster the *multivalent reading* (many-layered meanings) of a text.

In Britain the Venerable Bede (673–735) wrote a treatise, *Concerning Figures and Tropes*, that attempted to settle the questions regarding the difference between allegory as literary metaphor and as Christian occurrence, inventing the terms *allegoria in verbis* for the former and *allegoria in factis* for the latter, which reads various significations in the events of biblical "history." Language theory during this time and after studied *utterance* (spoken sounds), *ideation* (intellection), written *expression* (sounds and ideas as represented by alphabetical letters), and denotative *anchors* (the objective referents of written signs).

Various Arabic scholars, one of the earliest of whom was Al-Farabi (ca. 870–950), added Aristotle's *Rhetoric* and *Poetics* to the *Organon*, the categorical Arabic encyclopedia of Aristotle's texts on logic. This revised *compendium* emphasized the intellectual and technical side of rhetoric and poetry at the expense of content. Poetry was thus a division of logic, in the view of the later Arab scholar Averroes (1120–98), the art of *epideictic* (q.v.), that is, speeches of laudation or condemnation. The scholarship of these Arabs was highly influential in the West.

The father of modern literary criticism was Dante Alighieri (1265–1321), who managed to make a vernacular language, Italian, bear the weight that the classical languages had hitherto borne. Furthermore, he brought criticism to bear not only on the work of his contemporaries but on his own writings as well in order to justify them to the literate community for whom he wrote; whenever a writer stoops to criticism, it is for this purpose primarily. The poems of his *Vita Nuova* were written in verse and later glossed in prose in the exegetical manner of the *divisio textus* so as to expose the underlying meanings of the verses. The fragmentary *Convivio*, which Dante called a *comento* (commentary), had been planned as a sort of *accessus ad auctores* (introduction to authors) or allegorical interpretation of fourteen of his own *canzoni* (see *canzone* in *The Book of Forms*). These techniques themselves were methods the medieval biblical *exegete* applied as often as not in prefaces or introductions to the works of classical poets in the form of the *prologue paradigm* (*syllabus, outline*), discussing such topics as the biography and intentions of the poet, the bibliography, chronology, and quality of the work. By Dante's time the form of such prologues was this: (1) title of the work; (2) author; (3) author's intention; (4) content (*materia*); (5) method of treatment (*modus tractandi*) and usefulness of the treatise (*utilitas*); and (6) the category of the liberal arts and sciences under which the treatise fell (*cui parti philosophiae supponitur*). This form was supplanted by the *Aristotelian prologue*, the headings of which were *efficient cause* (*author*), *material cause* (*subject and treatment*), *formal cause* (*forma tractandi* or *literary form*), and *ultimate cause* (purpose, intention, usefulness).

Chaucer's French contemporary, the poet Eustache Deschamps (ca. 1346–ca. 1406) did a redaction in 1392 of the liberal arts *quadrivium* and *trivium* in his *L'Art de Dictier et de fere chançons*. The category of music he subdivided in two parts, *artificial music*, meaning instrumental or vocal musical sounds, and *natural music*, meaning poetry (*poiesis*), which he further classified as to poetic *formes fixes* (traditional verse forms), a service that George Puttenham (1530?–1590) would perform for the British in 1589 in his *Arte of English Poesie* and that *The Book of Forms* performs today.

The first British poet-critic was Philip Sidney (1554–86), author of *Apologie for Poetrie* (1595), which esteemed *praxis*, the practical utilization of knowledge, over *gnosis*, esoteric erudition. However, in Britain prior to the eighteenth century, Ben Jonson (ca. 1572–1637) stood as *exemplar* of the classical Aristotelian virtues by championing the mimetic nature of literature, its proportionate construction, and its emotional restraint. At this time literature was perceived as being written for a privileged educated public, and what criticism existed was aimed at that audience; but by the time that Joseph Addison (1672–1719) and Richard Steele (1672–1729) founded the literary periodical *The Tatler* (1709–11), literacy was much more widespread, and the editors chose to try to promote the values of a civilized society among a heterogeneous readership. The mission of their second magazine, *The Spectator* (1711-12) was expanded to include arbitration of the differences between the values of the burgeoning middle classes and those of the gentry, explaining notions of privilege and station to the former and of respectability and probity to the latter.

Alexander Pope (1688–1744), in his *Essay on Criticism*, was less interested in establishing the perimeters (not "parameters") of criticism than in explaining the function of the discipline as a tool for the inculcation of proper morals and civilized behavior. *Value theory,* or *axiology,* has four branches: *ethics*, the moral good; *politics*, the social good; *aesthetics*, the beautiful; and *pragmatics*, the useful. Samuel Johnson (1709–84) believed that "the end of writing is to instruct; the end of poetry is to instruct by pleasing," which is the feature that distinguishes belles lettres from other kinds of writing.

As the century wore on, these aspects of the function of criticism began to fade, and Sir Joshua Reynolds (1723–92) formulated the Augustan *normative,* or *perfectionist,* theory of mimetic art by once more mixing Platonism with Aristotelianism, postulating that an artist imitated no specific objects in Nature but rather *central forms,* which were *eidolons,* or ideal forms, of the *types* to be found in Nature; they were generalized therefrom by the *genius*, or exceptional creative power, of the individual artist. Genius is to be distinguished from *talent*, which is native ability: extraordinary natural aptitude for a given pursuit. A writer may have a talent, a *gift*, for words, but without genius, that writer will not rise to the level of *greatness*, to *Olympian heights*, the sphere of the gods. Such critical theory later came to be called *pre-Romantic*.

Expressive criticism views literature as the personal expression of the artist, and nineteenth-century Romantic theory postulated that poetry was the product of the genius, or *Great Poet,* who was possessed of greater *imagination* and *insight* than ordinary people because his (and presumably, her) moral *character* and *perception* was superior. John Henry Newman (1801–90) claimed that the Great Poet's *intuition* of "the *archetypes* of the beautiful" was essential to his genius. The Great Poets of the past were Homer (ca. 850 B.C.), Dante Alighieri, William Shakespeare (1564–1616), and John Milton; and in the Romantic period itself, William Wordsworth, who rejected Reynolds's system, postulating in its stead the view that nature ought to be interpreted realistically in poetry and art.

Poetry was capable of being studied and analyzed because it was as *sensible* as science; nevertheless, neither Romantic poets nor critics were much interested in intellectually exploring the subject of *form,* which would be determined by the action of the poet's imagination through *imagery* and *metered language (verse)*. The *style* of a poem would be determined by the ethical nature of the poet.

Poetry was considered to be the greatest of the arts; its object was the discovery and enunciation of *truth,* whose perceptible sign was *beauty*, as enunciated by John Keats (1795–1821): "'Beauty is truth, truth, beauty,'—that is all / Ye know on earth, and all ye need to know" ("Ode on a Grecian Urn"). Poetry must express great *ideas* and must have as its ultimate *object* the expression of a moral *viewpoint*, whatever its immediate *point* might be, and as its *material* the actual world—the *real* and the *factual*, the *corporeal* and the *spiritual*. The *subject matter* of poetry may be anything at all, as long as it is treated with *originality* and *sincerity*.

The third strain of Romantic critical theory after *Perfectionism* and *Realism* was Samuel Taylor Coleridge's *Idealism;* it too rejected Perfectionism but nevertheless maintained that the individualities expressed in poetry must also be representative of a class. A theory that took an even more Aristotelian viewpoint was *concrete idealism,* the foremost proponent of which was John Ruskin (1819–

1900). It looked to nature for its inspiration and duplicated it in language art. The truths of nature being *universal truths*—a term eventually replaced by *characteristic truth*—the poetry that best reproduces those truths is the greatest poetry.

Aubrey de Vere (1814–1902) categorized the kinds of *poetic truth* as the *truth of nature*, of character, of sentiment, of passion, of style, of diction, of observation, and of "keeping," which included the *architectonics* of the poem together with the *unity* of the poet's moral and intellectual *character*.

Many poets and critics in the nineteenth century, including Wordsworth and Coleridge, attempted to make distinctions between various related terms, including *imagination, fancy,* and *wit*. Imagination was the ability to think on a highly creative plane, conjuring images that made the world more intelligible or perceptible to the intelligence, whereas fancy was farther removed from reality, was more whimsical or playful or decorative. The *esemplastic*, according to Coleridge, is that imaginative ability of the poet to make an architectonic whole out of various and disparate elements. Wit was the ability to imagine or perceive incongruous connections between disparate things, as in the *pun* or the *bon mot*; it was the expression of the quick and humorously clever mind, but it was essentially superficial. If the pun is, as has often been claimed, "the lowest form of humor," what does that make William Shakespeare? He is the punster without peer in all of English literature. It is difficult to see how our greatest writer can also be our worst, but the Romantic and most of the Victorian poets and critics were nothing if not Transcendental philosophically—that is to say, Kantian and post-Kantian idealists and exceedingly earnest.

The Transcendentalist Ralph Waldo Emerson, who was the most influential American literary critic of the nineteenth century, borrowed three elements of British Romantic theory on which to construct his program regarding *organic poetry*: Coleridge's argument from *Biographia Literaria* (1817) regarding "Imagination"; Wordsworth's discussion in the Preface to the 1800 edition of *Lyrical Ballads* regarding the aesthetics of "Nature," and the thoughts of Thomas Carlyle (1795–1881) from *Sartor Resartus* (1832–33) regarding "Natural Supernaturalism." Briefly, American literature, particularly poetry, was not to rely on traditional literary forms and techniques, especially not those of the British, but upon *intuition*. The poem would choose its own form, like the shell being created by an unwitting snail or like the poems being created by Emerson's *exemplar*, Walt Whitman. Forgetting, perhaps, that he himself was writing criticism, Emerson claimed in his essay "The Poet," "Criticism is infested with a cant of materialism which assumes that manual skill and activity is the first merit of all men and disparages, such as say and do not, overlooking the fact that some men, namely poets, are natural sayers, sent into the world to the end of expression, and confounds them with those whose province is action but to quit it to imitate the sayers." In other words, poets are born, not made.

Whitman believed in *Personalism*, what would have been called "the cult of personality" in the cold war of the twentieth century, but it was his considered opinion that he was large enough of soul to stand not merely for the common man but for all men everywhere. Neither he nor Emerson (nor anyone else, apparently) claimed to stand for the common woman.

The second most important American critic of the nineteenth century, after Emerson, was Edgar Allan Poe, who influenced the French *Symbolists* (q.v.). Mystery remained an important element in poetry, but that mystery was to be achieved by using the discrete symbol, through *overtone*. The poet was to attempt thereby to achieve a glimpse of *supernal beauty,* which, though it sounded Transcendental, was not, for the most beautiful thing in the world was the death of a lovely woman. Poe was, in fact, an Aristotelian and a firm believer in poetic technique, as he showed in his essay "The Philosophy of Composition" (1846), wherein he explained how he composed his poem "The Raven." It was his opinion that any poem over one hundred lines in length was "a flat contradiction in terms," for *lyric intensity* could not be sustained that long. He was also at pains to dismiss the *"heresy of the didactic"* in poetry. Poe and Emerson were nearly diamectrical opposites in their literary views.

A late nineteenth-century French movement was *Aestheticism,* which in effect meant *"art for art's sake"* (*l'art pour l'art*), not for any *moral* or *didactic* sake (see *aesthetics,* below). This view eventually led to what has been called *decadence,* an art that grew out of *weltschmerz,* a German term meaning world-sickness, that is to say, jadedness and *ennui* such as that expressed vividly in T. S. Eliot's long *Modernist* poem, "The Waste Land." Another term associated with Aestheticism is the French *fin de siècle,* or end of the (nine-teenth) century, which, in Victorian times, had denoted a time of human progress on all fronts but which came to imply the *motif* of "the death of God"; the latter is expressed very well in W. B. Yeats's poem "The Second Coming" in which the *Millennium*—a cycle of a thousand years—is at hand and a new "saviour" is to be born. This poem is filled with quotable lines describing "the end of the cycle," including "Things fall apart; the centre cannot hold"; "The ceremony of innocence is drowned"; "And what rough beast, its hour come round at last, / Slouches towards Beth-lehem to be born?" It is a form of *eschatological poetry,* which is concerned with the end of the world, the Second Coming, judg-ment, resurrection, and the new world to come.

Late-nineteenth-century *Freudian critical theory* postulated that literary works betray the unconscious cravings of the authors. Such theory applied to an author's work was intended to produce a *psychobiography* but often produced only *psychobabble,* a term in-vented to describe the argot of psychiatry. Freudian *dream analysis,* part of the method of psychoanalysis, was in fact a form of literary criticism rather than the analysis of the unconscious mind, because the psychoanalyst could not become part of the mind of the dreamer so as to experience the dreams at firsthand; instead, all that could be analyzed was the *narrative* of the dream as related by the conscious dreamer, who could not be expected to remember the dream perfectly in its original form. The dreamer would thus be forced to select those dream events that were apprehensible, to put them into words, to arrange them in a more or less coherent order, and to convey them to the psychoanalyst at second hand. Another way of looking at it is this: writers were the original psychiatrists.

Modernist theory was primarily the work of Ezra Pound (1885–1972) and T. S. Eliot (1888–1965). It was the former who ranked types of criticism in a hierarchy of ascending importance: *criticism by discussion* included everything from fugitive reviewing to writing theoretical treatises; *criticism by translation* was the composition in one's own language of modern versions of ancient and foreign literature; *criticism by exercise in the style of a given period* was the reproduction in original works of the literary practices of historical periods; *criticism via music* was the exercise of *melopoiea* (lyricism) in original works; and finally, *criticism in new composition*, literary experimentation—it was Pound who sounded the Modernist watchword: "Make it new!" Clearly, Pound's ideal critic was a poet primarily, not a professional exegete or scholar.

T. S. Eliot's primary contribution to Modernist theory was his linkage of Modernist poetry with the poetry of the past, which, one would otherwise have thought, was exactly what high Modernists would want to eschew. Although it is true that the immediate effect of the Modernist revolt was to distance twentieth-century literature from that of the nineteenth century, particularly the Victorian era, Eliot made a case for a connection between his own work and the work of John Donne and the Metaphysical poets of the English Renaissance. His poem *The Waste Land* was the first major example of poetry written primarily, or very largely, in what has been called *abstract syntax* by Donald Davie (q.v., Bibliography), a path that would be more fully explored by Wallace Stevens (q.v.), but this feature of Eliot's poem was in fact brought to the fore by Pound's extensive revision of the original manuscript.

Aesthetics is the study of "beauty" in and of itself, separate from other considerations, such as ethics, morality, and so forth. A number of critics, writers, and *littérateurs,* including T. S. Eliot among the moderns and Aristotle among the ancients, have maintained that the *creative nature* is composed of two elements, *emotion* and *intellect*. If in the creator of art there is a cleavage between the two and a too heavy emphasis placed on one or the other, a *dissociation of sensibility* takes place, Eliot maintained, and poetic imbalance occurs. Verse too much of the mind is *verse essay*, not poetry, and verse too much of the emotions is mere *confession* or *effusion*. Wordsworth, attempting to strike a balance between these views, believed that poetry is "emotion recollected in tranquility," and Keats invented the term *negative capability* to express something like the same thing: the ability of the poet to assume a mask in order to see with another's eyes, not one's own.

Aesthetic distance—a term adopted by the *neo-Aristotelian, objective, practical criticism of the Chicago School* and *the New Criticism,* which flourished from the 1920s through World War II and into the mid-century (a synonym is *psychic distance*)—means the severance of oneself from the object being evaluated so as to be able to consider it objectively, without *bias* and without *prior assumptions*, as in the commission of the *intentional fallacy*, which is the critical error of attempting to understand a literary work by accepting at face value an author's statement of what he or she intended to accomplish in it or by inferring the author's intention from the work itself or from some other source, such as the life of the author. The *biographical fallacy* is the error of judging something by referring it to the author's life story, for works of literature may or may not be "about" an author's experiences. Likewise, the *historical fallacy* is the attempt to read into a work of literature something of the times during which it was written, which may or may not have anything to do with the case.

The *affective fallacy* is a New Critical term meaning the error of judging a work of literature by the emotional effect it has upon the reader. The *egopoetic fallacy*, of which Whitman was guilty, is the belief on the part of a writer that his or her autobiographical experiences have universal significance in and of themselves, resulting in a hyperromantic *dissociation of sensibility* and diminution of *aesthetic distance* between the writer, his or her *artifice*, and the *audience*.

On the other hand, all of these "fallacies" are also critical "systems." Eneas Sweetland Dallas, in his 1852 "Poetics: An Essay on Poetry," called for a *comparative criticism*:

The comparison required is threefold; the first, which most persons would regard as in a peculiar sense critical, a comparison of all the arts one with another, as they appear together and in succession; the next, psychological, a comparison of these in their different phases with the nature of the mind, its intellectual bias and its ethical needs as revealed in the latest analysis; the third, historical, a comparison of the results thus obtained with the facts of history, the influence of race, of religion, of climate, in one word, with the story of human development.

Biographical criticism studies a writer's work in relation to his or her life; *historical criticism* (including *antiquarianism* and *chronologism*) judges the work in its historical context (see *New Historicism*, below); *subjective criticism* (*impressionistic criticism*) approaches the work from the viewpoint of the critic's personal impressions—a contemporary school is called *reader response* criticism (q.v., below). *Comparative criticism* compares and contrasts different works or different authors. *Heuristics* is a course of investigation undertaken by some particular means leading to discovery; for instance, searching for archetypes in a genre such as *matriarchal literature*.

The Swiss linguist Ferdinand de Saussure (1857–1913) coined the term *structuralism* and argued the ambiguity of language signs, which he divided into the *signifier* (the word itself) and the *signified* (the concept behind the word). He maintained that any word could stand for any object or concept and had meaning only through social convention, an unarguable position, as anyone who has tried to learn a foreign language will testify. Of course, every signifier will have a history often stretching back into dim antiquity, and its *etymology* can usually be traced, together with its changes, or *transformations*, which is what the science of *linguistics* examines. Thus, each signifier defines itself by its *difference* from every other signifier, and the same is true of every signified within the field of the language in question and not through any connection with the thing or concept it purports to represent. The field of linguistics is split between those who believe in *hypotaxis*, the theory that language is subsumed by the science of language, or in *parataxis*, the theory which posits that language and its science are separate entities.

Postmodernism is a term that means at least two things: a reaction by writers against the principles of Modernism and a turning away from radical literary experimentation toward the reintroduction of traditional standards and devices or, contrarily, an attempt to carry to extremes the principles of Modernism. Postmodernism also shows a propensity by critics and scholars to turn away from literature toward criticism itself, specifically critical theory, and to treat critical texts as more important than or at least as important as the literary texts that criticism traditionally had existed to explicate and examine. To this end, certain critical schools have attempted to *deconstruct* the literary *text* so that it becomes a meaningless object. Unfortunately, in doing so, critics have assured their own self-destruction or at least marginalization, since the only readers of such texts are other critics who enjoy the manipulation of their abstruse *argot* (q.v.). The term *Poststructuralism* stands in relation to *Structuralism* as the term *Postmodernism* stands to *Modernism*; that is to say, it refers to those *critical theories* that follow Structuralism and either oppose or extend its premises.

Deconstruction, a term coined by the French critic Jacques Derrida during the 1960s, is a theory of literary criticism based on the "difference," postulated by Saussure, that disputes the critical assumption that language can carry meaning in and of itself. Words have reference only to other words and not to objects or ideas: "In deconstruction, the critic claims there is no meaning to be found in the actual text, but only in the various, often mutually irreconcilable, 'virtual texts' constructed by readers in their search for meaning," according to Rebecca Goldstein. One of the techniques used by such critics to prove that words undermine one another is the identification of *binary oppositions* within a text to show, first, that there is a *hierarchy of terminology* ("John saw the world in terms of **black and white**"); second, the inversion of the hierarchy in order to reverse the meaning of the original terms ("John saw the world in terms of **white and black**"); and, third, the neutralization of both terms nonhierarchically ("John saw the world in terms of **whack**"). In this case, the neutralization is a *portmanteau word* (q.v.).

J. Douglas Kneale declares that "reading is an act that critics perform vis-à-vis texts but also something that texts perform on themselves in those moments when they declare and at the same time dispute their status as language." But this statement—if one understands its meaning—is like Emerson's regarding the ability of the poem to choose its own form, for "texts" cannot perform anything "on" themselves because they are not sentient. Everything "in" a text occurs not in the text but in the mind of the reader. A mind duplicates, or attempts to duplicate, what occurred in the mind of a writer as it is reflected in a text. Furthermore, if a text deconstructs itself and therefore has no meaning, then there is no point in reading literature or in writing criticism, for it is meaningless, like all other texts, like this text.

Reader-response theory (*reader theory, response theory*) posits that the reader is actively involved with the text, which in and of itself is not a self-contained whole. The reader may in fact be a character in the text, like the *narrator*, but as a *narratee,* or receiver of the narration, who may be addressed by the narrator as in Victorian novels: "Dear Reader, bear with me as we begin this tale of adventure and woe, for in the end you may be both surprised and mollified." Furthermore, the reader will actively fill in hiatuses and ellipses in the narration and make particular assumptions about meanings and situations that will not be shared by any other reader, and the author will be deliberately manipulating the reactions and responses of the reader by means of various devices. Much of the story takes place not on the page but in the mind of the reader, who will, in any case, bring a particular perspective to bear on the text and will read it in terms of that perspective (i.e., the perspective of a Christian, of a prude, of a sadist, and so on and so forth). In each case, the effect of the text on the reader will be different, though everyone will read the "same" story.

Liberation criticism is an umbrella term that covers those critical theories that have arisen from the counterculture movements of the 1960s. These approaches include *gay criticism* ("*queer theory*"), *ecological* (or *Gaia*) *theory, antiwar* and *ban-the-bomb, Black* and *Hispanic, Marxist-Leninist,* and *feminist* (including *Lesbian*) *criticism.* These and later theories, such as *postcolonialist* and *multiculturalist criticism,* during the 1990s were assembled under the rubric of *politically correct theory.*

Feminist theory, which began in *consciousness-raising* confrontation sessions, is too wide and diverse to summarize adequately in a short space. Some of the issues that are of literary importance have to do with the discovery and publication of neglected women writers of the past in order to provide a context of literary and role models, canonicity, and viewpoint; the establishment of women's studies, or *feminology,* in a paternalist society; and the encouragement and development of new women writers. Like all other schools of twentieth-century critical theory, feminists have formed alliances with and experienced the permutations of other critical systems, including those of Marxists, structuralists, deconstructionists, poststructuralists, Gaia theorists, and so on. The critics who have emerged from these circumstances have been dubbed *gynocritics* by Elaine Showalter. Finally, *the New Historicism* maintains that each individual event, including the written text, takes place not *in vacuo* but in a cultural and historical environment and that no event or text, therefore, may be studied apart from its interactive context.

CHAPTER GLOSSARY

Italicized terms are glossed elsewhere in the book; see index.

ABBREVIATION. A shortening of a commonly understood word or phrase, for instance, *etc.* for the Latin *et cetera;* also a symbol that stands for a word or phrase, for instance, *ampersand* (&) for "and."

ABBREVIATIONS. Some common abbreviations used in literary works are *aet.* or *aetat.* (for *aetatis suae*) meaning "aged," as in "He died *aetat.* thirty-five." *Ibid.* (*ibidem*) means "This quotation is to be found in the same work as the last quotation noted," as in a second or later reference to the same work in a series of footnotes. A term that is sometimes confused with *ibid.* is *idem*, which is not an abbreviation; it means "This has been cited previously." *Op. cit.* (*opere citato*) means "in the work cited," as in a second quotation chosen from a work previously cited. *Ca.* or simply the letter *c.* means *circa*, Latin for "around" or "thereabout," as in "John Doe was born ca. 1910."

ABECEDARIUM. See *primer*.

ABRIDGEMENT. A shortening or condensation of a literary work, as distinguished from an unabridged work published as written by the original author. See *editor*.

ABSTRACT. A summary of the most significant points of a text.

ABSTRACTION. A word or verbal construct that represents an idea rather than a thing; the opposite of *concretion*. See *reification* and *symbol*.

ABSTRACT NOUN. A word that signifies an idea rather than a thing.

ACADEMIC, ACADEMIC PRESS. See *publishing* and *scholar*.

ACADEMICIAN. A member of the faculty of a school, college, or university. See *scholar*.

ACYRON. Use of words inappropriate to the thing being described; mixed metaphor. See *catachresis*.

AD, ADVERTISEMENT. See *propaganda*.

ALIAS. See *pseudonym*.

ALLEGORICAL INTERPRETATION. The symbolic level of any text. See *senses of interpretation*.

ALLEGORY. See *senses of interpretation*.

ALLONYM. See *pseudonym*.

ALMANAC. A yearly publication containing all sorts of agricultural information, including such things as the phases of the moon, weather forecasts, riddles, games—things that farmers can use in their work and during the winter months when, traditionally, there is little to do on a farm. Modern almanacs are often miniature encyclopedias.

ALTERNATIVE PRESS. See *publishing*.

AMBIGUITY (or *plurisignation*). Multiple or polysemous meaning, the allowance of overtone and *connotation* by *context*. William Empson (q.v., Bibliography) has identified "seven types of ambiguity"

(1) First type ambiguities arise when a detail is effective in several ways at once, e.g., by comparisons with several points of likeness, antitheses with several points of difference, "comparative" adjectives, subdued metaphors, and extra meanings suggested by rhythm. (2) . . . two or more alternative meanings are fully resolved into one. (3) . . . two apparently unconnected meanings are given simultaneously. (4) . . . the alternative meanings combine to make clear a complicated state of mind in the author. (5) . . . a fortunate confusion, as when the author is discovering his idea in the act of writing . . . or not holding it all at once. (6) . . . what is said is contradictory or irrelevant and the reader is forced to invent interpretations. (7) . . . full contradiction, marking a division in the author's mind.

See also *energia*.

AMPHIBOLOGY, AMPHIBOLY. A remark that can be taken in two ways; *double entendre*. See *ambiguity*.

ANA. A collection of odds and ends, curiosities and intelligence, gossip and anecdote, having to do with a particular subject. It is most often to be encountered as a suffix, as in "Johsoni**ana**," a collection of materials having to do with Samuel Johnson.

ANAGOGE. See *senses of interpretation*.

ANAGOGICAL INTERPRETATION. The spiritual level of any text. See *senses of interpretation*.

ANALECT. Selected portions of a work of literature or set of works. Analects (*analecta*) are gleanings or extracts from the work of an author. See *ana* and *anthology*.

ANCHORED ABSTRACTION. The equation of an abstract noun with a concrete noun, thus defining the abstraction, for instance, "Love is a puppy." See *symbol*.

ANGST A feeling of trepidation or dread often accompanied by despondency. Although it is derived from an old German word, it is a term that is associated with Freudian psychology, existential philosophy, and *theater of the absurd*.

ANNA. Yearly records, like the proceedings of a scholarly or professional group or *The Anglo-Saxon Chronicle*.

ANNOTATED BIBLIOGRAPHY. See *notes*.

ANNUAL. A book of any type that is published yearly, such as a college *yearbook*.

ANOPISTHOGRAPH. See *printing*.

ANTHOLOGIST. The *editor* of an *anthology*.

ANTHOLOGY. A collection of stories, poems, or nonfiction pieces by more than one author, a miscellany, omnium-gatherum, or *compendium*.

APERÇU. A synopsis of a work. For a second meaning, see *epiphany*.

APOCALYPTIC LITERATURE. Literature that is prophetic of the end of the world.

APOCRYPHA. Books of the Bible that are not accepted as canonical, but in a broader sense they are works attributed to a writer without final proof of authorship, such as the apocryphal plays of Shakespeare.

APPENDIX. Supplemental material added to the end of a volume, sometimes an excursus, a formal digression or detailed discussion of an ancillary (secondary) point made in the body of the book. See *journal* and *notes*.

ARCHITECTONICS. The overall structure of a literary work.

ARTIFICE, ARTIFICIAL. See *tautologia*.

ARTISTIC MERIT. See *censor, censorship* and taste, under *tautologia*.

AUDIENCE. The vertical audience is a group of readers that exists at a particular moment in history; the horizontal audience is a group of readers that exists from a particular moment in history forward through time; the *contemporary audience* is a group of readers that exists at the same time as a particular writer.

AUFKLÄRUNG. A critical synonym for the Enlightenment, borrowed from the German. See literary periods in the chapter on the discipline of literature.

AUTHOR. The creator of written material.

AUTOGRAPH. The signature of an author on a copy of a book by that author. See *holograph* and *printing*.

AUTOTELIC. A term from the New Criticism, meaning a work of art that is self-referential, needing no external reason for being other than itself. It is the opposite of *didactic*.

BACONIAN THEORY. See *bardolatry*.

BARDOLATRY. The worship of poets; specifically, of Shakespeare. Those who cannot bear the thought that a *paideia*, an outlander of little education, could have written so well and so prolifically resort to *Baconian theory*—the idea that Francis Bacon, the great essayist and thinker of the Renaissance in England, was the actual author of the plays and poems. A recent development along these lines is the contemporary society known as the Tremblestick League, which argues that the works of Shakespeare were actually written by Bill Tremblestick, a janitor of the Globe Theatre. This organization has called for a fifty-year moratorium on all things Shakespearian, including productions and all sorts of scholarship—niggling *pedantry*, criticism, conjecture, and so forth—so that the matter may be studied without distraction. During the interim the plays of Shakespeare's contemporaries, including Thomas Kyd, Christopher Marlowe, and Ben Jonson, may be performed.

BAROQUE. See *tautologia*.

BIBLE. See *bibliomancy* and *apocrypha*. See also *heuristics* in text.

BIBLIOCLASM, BIBLIOCLAST. A biblioclast is one who destroys books; a biblioclasm is a book burning.

BIBLIOFILM. See *microfilm*.

BIBLIOGRAPHY. See *notes*.

BIBLIOLATRY. The worship of books.

BIBLIOMANCY. A form of prophecy that uses the Bible as its oracle: one opens the pages of the Good Book and points one's fingers randomly at a passage that will be magically apropos.

BIBLIOMANIA. An obsession with the collecting of books.

BIBLIOPHILIA. Love of books.

BIBLIOPHOBIA. A fear of books.

BIBLIOTHERAPY, BIBLIOTHERAPIST. Bibliotherapy is the use of literature (stories, poems, plays) as a type of treatment for psychological disorders, and a bibliotherapist is a specialist in this sort of approach.

BILL. A legislative document to be considered for enactment.

BINDING. See *bookbinding*.

BIOGRAPHY. See the chapter "The Genres of Nonfiction."

BLACK LETTER, BLACK LETTER BOOK. See *printing*.

BLEED, BLEED OFF, BLEED PAGE. See *printing*.

BLOCK BOOK. See *printing*.

BLURB. See *notes*.

BODY. See *book*.

BOOK. A group of pages or leaves bound together as a unit. See *bookbinding*, *publishing*, and *script*.

BOOKBINDING. The same materials that were used as *writing surfaces* were often used for bookbinding: a full binding is one that is made completely of some sort of leather; a quarter-binding, of leather with paper corners; half-binding, of leather with paper corners and spine. The spine of a book is the bound edge of the pages; the fore-edge is the opposite unbound edge of the book, and the other edges are called simply top edge and bottom edge. All edges might be gilt. The *covers*, front and back, complete the binding; they might be made of stiff, limp, or plush material.

Endpapers are double-width pages glued to the inside front or back covers of a book and attached to the first or last pages. The flyleaf is a blank initial or final page of the book. The front or righthand side of a page (the odd page) is the recto, and the back or lefthand side (the even page) is the verso.

BOOK BURNING. See *biblioclasm*.

BOOK DESIGN. See *printing*.

BOOK OF HOURS. See *breviary*.

BOOK REVIEW. See *secondary source*.

BOTTOM EDGE. See *bookbinding*.

BOWDLERIZATION. See *condensation*.

BREVIARY. A book that contains the offices, prayers, and hymns for the canonical hours; a book of hours.

BRIEF. A compressed document or series of documents, a *condensation*.

BROADSHEET, BROADSIDE, BROADSIDE BALLAD. A broadside or broadsheet is a single sheet of paper ordinarily printed on one side only. Broadside ballads were song lyrics or verses printed on single sheets, originally sold in in the streets and usually illustrated by woodcuts.

BROCHURE. See *books*.

BULL, BULLETIN. A bull is an official document stating a doctrine or credo; a paper of less weight is a bulletin.

CALLIGRAPHY. Fine lettering. See *documentation*.

CAPTION. See *books*.

CARBON COPY. See *script*.

CAST TYPE. See *printing*.

CATACHRESIS. A term that implies misuse of tropes, as in the mixed metaphor; see also *acyron*.

CATECHISM. A short book containing a summary, in pregunta (requesta, question; respuesta, answer) form, of the doctrine of the Christian church.

CENSOR, CENSORSHIP. Biblioclasm and iconoclasm are only one step removed from censorship, the repression or banning of books or other written documents containing material someone objects to for one arbitrary reason or another, such as a judgment that the work is pornography: sexually explicit writing that is deemed by the censors to have no artistic merit. See also *condensation*.

CHAPBOOK, CHAPMAN. A chapbook ("cheap book") is the original paperback: a pamphlet or brochure containing a few pages of poetry, fiction, or other materials, such as religious tracts, bound usually only in wrappers, stiffer paper or cardboard. Originally sold by street hawkers called chapmen.

CHAPTER, CHAPTER HEADING. A section of a book is a chapter, and its heading or title is a rubric or caption.

CHRESTOMATHY. Either an anthology of literary pieces used in learning a language or a collection of pieces by a single author.

CHRONICLE. See *ana*.

CLOSE READING. Literary analysis. See *exegesis*.

CODEX, CODICES. See *documentation*.

COFFEE-TABLE BOOK. A modern illustrated text, often printed on extra-large pages, designed to be seen lying on a table in a home as part of the décor.

COGNITIVE MEANING. See *reification*.

COLLABORATION. See *pseudonym*.

COLLATION. A scholarly comparison of the various editions of a text or of an author's works, with an eye to the publication of a definitive edition or recension of that text or that author's *oeuvre*. See *secondary source*.

COLOPHON. See *printing*.

COMMENTATOR. See *documentation*.

COMMONPLACE BOOK. See *journal*.

COMPENDIUM, COMPILATION. A gathering of various written materials. See *anthology*, *compiler*, and *editor*.

COMPILER. An *anthologist* or *editor*. See *documentation*.

CONCRETE NOUN. A word that signifies a thing rather than an idea.

CONCRETION. A word or verbal construct that represents a thing rather than an idea; the opposite of abstraction. See *reification* and *symbol*.

CONDENSATION. A conspectus is an overall survey of a subject, whereas an epitome is a summary of the essence of a piece, like the précis, which is a concise summation of a text that retains something of the flavor of the original. A redaction is an edited version of a work; a synopsis is an overview or outline of a work, and a résumé is the summary of a work or case. A digest is a collection of previously published materials that have been edited and condensed. A bowdlerization (after Thomas Bowdler, 1754–1825) is an expurgation, that is, a prudishly edited (bowdlerized) or *censored* version of a work. See also *brief*.

CONNOTATION. A secondary definition of a word, *overtone*. See *energia*.

CONSPECTUS. See condensation.

CONTEMPORARY AUDIENCE. See *audience*.

CONTEXT. The immediate environment of a word in a phrase, clause, sentence, paragraph, and so forth. See *energia*.

CONVENTIONAL DEFINITION. The definition of a word that has been generally agreed on; see *denotation*.

COPY. See *carbon copy, documentation,* and *photocopy*.

COPYEDIT. See *script*.

COPYIST. See *documentation* and *scribe*.

COPYRIGHT. See *printing*.

COURTESY BOOK. A medieval volume, generally written in dialogue, explaining the rules of chivalry governing knights, as in the courts of love.

COVER. See *bookbinding*.

CS, CS, CSS. See *script*.

DATE OF PUBLICATION. See *printing*.

DECKLED EDGE. See *printing*.

DECORUM. The suitability of an element of a literary work, such as tone or *style*, to its specific environment or to the work as a whole, its *architectonics*.

DEFINITIVE EDITION. See *collation*.

DEGREE OF ARTIFICE. See *tautologia*.

DENOTATION. The primary definition of a word.

DESKTOP PUBLICATION. See *publishing*.

DIARY. See *journal*.

DIDACTIC. Instructive, teaching morality.

DIGEST. See *condensation*.

DIGRESSION. See *appendix*.

DISSERTATION. See *document*.

DIVINE FORCE. See *instress*.

DOCUMENT, DOCUMENTATION. A document is any written material that can be used to provide evidence; documentation is the providing of evidence in a treatise or other formal scholarly essay, such as a monograph or dissertation: a book-length essay on a particular subject.

A primary source is the original place from which scholarship is derived, such as the original *manuscript* or typescript of a novel, or the first printing of a poem in a periodical. A *secondary source* is any document or other material that is once removed from the primary source, such as an account by a later writer of a manuscript or publication.

A handwritten book or other text is a *manuscript* (often given in abbreviated form as MS or ms; plural, mss), and sometimes called a codex (plural, *codices*), either a *holograph manuscript* by the *author*, or a copy made by a copyist, such as a *scribe* (a master of *calligraphy*, beautiful *handwriting* or *script*), a public clerk, or a *scrivener*.

Other kinds of "authors" are the *compiler*, which we would now call an *editor*, and the commentator, like the rabbi who studies and writes about the Torah and Jewish law.

DRAMATIC PROPRIETY. A judgment as to whether a speech or an action in a literary work is appropriate, not to the real world but to the situation that exists within the work itself.

DUODECIMO. See *printing*.

DUST JACKET. The protective outer covering of a book. A slipcover or slipcase is a heavier shield, often a box with the fore-edge open so that the volume may be slipped inside.

EDGE. See *bookbinding*.

EDITION. See *printing*.

EDITOR. One who works with and emends the writings of authors.

EISEGESIS. A form of empathy, in effect reading one's own voice into a text.

EMBLEM. See *symbol*.

EMBLEM BOOK. A collection of mottos, each of which is preceded by a brief poem illustrative of the motto.

EMENDATION. The correction of faulty written materials. See *editor*.

EMOTIVE MEANING. The emotional effect of a word or a text as distinguished from its intellectual or rational effect. See *reification*; see also cue in text.

ENCOMIUM. See *festschrift*.

ENDPAPER. See *bookbinding*.

ENERGIA. The meanings or the sense of literature (see *senses of interpretation*). Every text must make "sense," not necessarily logical sense but, in context, poetic sense. If a metaphor or other *trope* makes no sense of any kind, for instance, where the *context* does not block out enough *connotations* and there is confusion about what a word means (it may mean too many things, at which point *ambiguity* becomes *obscurity*), then the trope is catachretic or *acyron* is present (see *catachresis*).

EPIGRAPH. See *notes*.

EPIPHANY. In literature, the sudden revelation of the meaning of something, an *aperçu*; epiphanous stories, such as those having to do with growing up into the adult world, deal with the revelatory nature of what it means to be no longer a child or an innocent.

EPITOME. See *condensation*.

EPONYM. See *pseudonym*.

ETIQUETTE BOOK. A Renaissance handbook covering the rules of polite conduct in upper-class society. Modern etiquette books do the same for middle-class society.

EUHEMERISM. The theory that *myth* may be elucidated through historical study or by an examination of its objectives or motivations ; see also *archetype*.

EXARGASIA. Polish, smoothness of surface, and intricacy of language texture.

EXCLUSION. The deletion of multiple meanings. See *obscurity*.

EXCURSUS. See *appendix*.

EXEGESIS. Another term for *explication* of a text through *close reading* and literary analysis of the forms and meanings of language.

EXPLICATION. See *exegesis*.

EXPURGATION. See *condensation*.

FACE. See *printing*.

FACSIMILE, FAX. A copy of a text transmitted by telephone line. See also *printing*.

FESTSCHRIFT. An anthology of pieces by various authors published as an encomium to a writer or to an honored scholar.

FIGMENT. See *idolum*.

FIGURE OF SPEECH. A description, analogy, metaphor, or rhetorical trope; see tropes in *The Book of Forms*.

FIRST EDITION, FIRST PRINTING. See *documentation* and *printing*.

FLYLEAF. See *bookbinding*.

FOLIO. See *printing*.

FONT, FONT STYLE. See *printing*.

FOOTNOTE. See *notes*.

FORE-EDGE. See *bookbinding*.

FOREWORD. See *introduction*.

FORMAT. See *printing*.

FOUL COPY, FOUL PROOF. See *script*.

FULL BINDING. See *bookbinding*.

GEORGICS. See *handbook*.

GHOST WRITER. See *pseudonym*.

GIFT BOOK. Especially in the nineteenth century, a very fancy edition of some sort, often with plush or limp covers, gilt edges, a ribbon bookmark and an inscription page; see *bookbinding*.

GILT. See *bookbinding* and *manuscript*.

GLOSS, GLOSSARY. See *notes*.

HAGIOGRAPHY. The biography of a saint.

HALF-BINDING. See *bookbinding*.

HALF TITLE. See *printing*.

HANDBOOK. A handy reference work dealing with a particular subject, like georgics, versified handbooks in the trades and crafts, and like the volume currently in your hand.

HANDWRITING. Script, calligraphy. See *documentation*.

HEADING. See *chapter heading*.

HEADNOTE. See *notes*.

HECTOGRAPH. See *printing*.

HOLOGRAPH. The handwriting of the author of a text. See *documentation*.

HORIZONTAL AUDIENCE. See *audience*.

HORNBOOK. See *primer*.

ICONOCLAST. A relative of the *biblioclast*, originally one who destroyed religious images, but in modern times the word means merely one who attacks and attempts to destroy ideas, particularly popular ones.

IDEATION. Thought, intellectuation, ratiocination, rationalization.

IDOLUM (plural, *idola*). A figment of the imagination, a mental image.

ILLUMINATED MANUSCRIPT. See *manuscript*.

IMAGE. See *figure of speech, idolum, trope,* and *symbol*.

IMPRIMATUR. A *nihil obstat* (no objection) license to print issued by a church official.

IMPRINT. See *printing*.

INCLUSION. The presence of multiple meanings. See *ambiguity* and *energia*.

INCUNABLE, INCUNABULA, INCUNABULUM. See *printing*.

INDEX (plural, *indices*). A full list of terms, names, or other important items in the body of the book; it is to be found at the end of the book.

INDEX LIBRORUM PROHIBITORUM. The official list of Roman Catholic banned books.

INITIALS. See *manuscript*.

INSCAPE. A term invented by Gerard Manley Hopkins, it is the inherent nature of a thing, as perceived by the writer and expressed in words.

INSTRESS. Another Hopkins term: the divine force that creates the inscape and enables the writer to perceive it.

INTRODUCTION. May be a foreword, a prefatory note or preamble, or a full preface, a prolegomenon (plural, prolegomena).

JESTBOOK, JOKEBOOK. A volume full of jokes, humorous anecdotes, ribaldries, and so forth; since the nineteenth century, called a jokebook.

JOTTINGS. See *journal*.

JOURNAL. A diary is a personal journal in which the occurrences of one's life are entered at regular intervals, to be distinguished from a commonplace book, which is a notebook containing jottings of one sort or another: ideas, memoranda (singular, memorandum; shorthand, memo) or reminders, quotations from reading sources, and the like.

JUVENILIA. The earliest writings of an author.

LACUNA. See *manuscript*.

LAYOUT. See *printing*.

LEAF. See *printing*.

LEMMA. A caption or motto attached to a picture.

LETTERING. See *printing*.

LETTERPRESS. See *printing*.

LIMITED EDITION. See *printing*.

LITERAL INTERPRETATION. The surface or narrative level of a text. See *senses of interpretation*.

LITERARY ANALYSIS. See *exegesis*.

LITERARY QUARTERLY. See *periodicals*.

LITTLE MAGAZINE. See *periodicals*.

LOGICAL SENSE. See *energia*.

MANUSCRIPT. An illuminated manuscript is a book that has been copied, often by a monk in a medieval monastery, and ornamented with colored initials (the initial letters of sentences or paragraphs) and other illustrations and adornments, often in gilt or gold leaf. A lacuna is a portion of a manuscript that is missing owing to a lost page or series of pages, a tear, a blot, or some other problem. A reconstruction is a scholarly restoration of the material lost in the lacuna. See *documentation*.

MARGIN, MARGINALIA. See *notes*.

MEMO, MEMORANDA, MEMORANDUM. See *journal*.

MICROFICHE, MICROFILM. Reduced photocopies of texts and documents stored on film or on cards that can be enlarged and scanned by reading machines. Bibliofilm is a type of microfilm material that is used to photograph and preserve the pages of books and other written or drawn works.

MIMEOGRAPH. See *printing*.

MISCELLANY. See *anthology*.

MIXED METAPHOR. See *acyron*, *catachresis*, and *energia*.

MONOGRAPH. See *document*.

MOTTO. See *lemma*.

MOVABLE TYPE. See *printing*.

NIHIL OBSTAT. See *imprimatur*.

NOM DE PLUME. See *pseudonym*.

NOTATIONS. See *notes*. Also see *notation* in *The Book of Forms*.

NOTEBOOK. See *journal*.

NOTES. A gloss is a note of explanation; a collection of such notes is called a glossary. Other sorts of notes include marginalia or scholia, notations written by a *scholiast* in the margin, the blank border surrounding a text. The headnote is an epigraph or a texte (quotation from an appopriate source) or other preceding explanation; and the footnote, a notation at the bottom of the page.

A blurb or puff is a quotation by someone lauding a book, printed on the *dust jacket* of that book. A bibliography is a list of books on a particular subject, and an annotated bibliography is a list that has been glossed.

NUMBERING. See *printing*.

OBSCURITY. Blocked meaning, *exclusion* of sense, in that the ordinary sense of a text has been excluded. See *energia*.

OCTAVO. See *printing*.

OEUVRE. The complete works of an author.

OFFSET PRESS. See *printing*.

OMNIUM-GATHERUM. See *anthology*.

PAIDEIA. An unworthy person or writer.

PALIMPSEST. See *writing surfaces*.

PAMPHLET. See *books*.

PAPER. See *writing surfaces*.

PAPYRUS. See *writing surfaces*.

PARADIGM. The model for something; a list of the inflections of a word that stands as a model for the category of declensions or conjugations of its type.

PARADOX. A metaphor or statement that combines terms that seem mutually exclusive but in fact are not. Such locutions often exhibit *plurisignation*, simultaneous meanings.

PARAGON. An example without peer, as in "Keats' ode is a paragon of the poetic art." See *paradigm*.

PARCHMENT. See *writing surfaces*.

PEDANTRY. A show of erudition, niggling scholarship.

PEN NAME. See *pseudonym*.

PERIODICALS. A slick is a periodical with a glossy cover, usually issued monthly; a pulp is a magazine printed on the cheapest possible paper (manufactured from pulpwood), generally matched by the contents. A *little magazine*, on the other hand, is one that publishes fiction and poetry, generally; despite limited circulations, often under one thousand copies in a run, some little magazines have been responsible for bringing to light many of the major talents of the literary world both in Britain and the United States. Literary quarterlies are noted for publishing creative writing and also for nonfiction, scholarship, and criticism; many are affiliated with academic institutions. See *books*.

PHOTOCOPY. A copy of a text made by photography. See also *microfiche* and *microfilm*.

PICTOGRAPH. A picture that is representative of something. See *symbol*.

PIRATED EDITION. See *printing*.

PLAGIARISM. Literary theft, the use of another writer's material without giving written credit for such use at least in some sort of note and, in the case of copyrighted material, without applying for and receiving *permission* to use it.

PLURISIGNATION. Multiple meanings of a single word.

POETIC PASSAGE. A poetic passage is a portion of a prose work such as a novel or short story where the narrative stops and the author begins to use the language to build a word picture, as in that portion of Nathaniel Hawthorne's story "Rapaccini's Daughter" where the poisonous garden is described in poetic prose. Such a passage overdone is a purple patch (see *purple prose*).

POETIC PROSE. See *poetic passage*.

POETIC SENSE. See *energia*.

POLYSEMOUS MEANING. See *ambiguity* and *plurisignation*.

PORNOGRAPHY. See *censor, censorship*.

PREAMBLE. See *introduction*.

PRÉCIS. See *condensation*.

PREFACE, PREFATORY NOTE. See *introduction*.

PREGUNTA. See *catechism*.

PRESS RUN. See *printing*.

PRIMARY SOURCE. See *documentation*.

PRIMER. The first schoolbook, an *abecedarium*. A hornbook is a primer on paper or vellum covered with a sheet of transparent horn to protect it from wear and grime.

PRINTING. An anopisthograph, or block-book, is a book printed from engraved blocks of wood, a method of publication that preceded the invention of cast type by Johannes Gutenberg (1400?–1468?) in or about the year 1455. An incunabulum (incunable; plural, incunabula) is a book printed from movable type before the year 1501. Black letter refers to a type of heavy, angular Gothic font style in which early printed books were often produced, and a black-letter book means, in effect, such a volume. A font is one complete set of type of a single size and face.

A leaf is a sheet of paper, and a folio is a leaf folded once at the center, making a signature, or gathering, of four pages of a book or manuscript, each page generally about fifteen inches tall. A quarto is such a sheet of paper folded twice, to make a signature of four leaves or eight pages; an octavo is a sheet folded into a signature of eight leaves, or sixteen pages; a duodecimo (twelvemo or 12mo) is twelve leaves, twenty-four pages. There are also signatures of sixteenmo (16mo), thirty-twomo (32mo) and sixty-fourmo (64mo).

Such pages are printed first, then folded, then *trimmed* before binding; that is, the folded edges are cut so that they may be opened. A book that has been bound without being trimmed is said to be *uncut* or *unopened*. Books printed on handmade paper whose uneven upper or lower edges have not been trimmed are said to have deckled edges. If a book is trimmed in such a way as to cut off part of an illustration or so as to leave no margin between the illustration and the edge of the page, the illustration bleeds off, and the page is a bleed page.

An edition of a book is all copies printed from a single typesetting. A limited edition is a press run of a particular number of copies, each copy numbered or lettered and perhaps *autographed* by the author, usually printed letterpress, that is, on a press utilizing metal type set by hand or machine rather than by computer or digital methods, as distinguished from other types of printing processes, such as rotary, rotogravure, offset, mimeograph, hectograph, and so forth. A subsequent run from the same type is called a second (third, fourth) printing, but only the first printing is considered a first edition. A *facsimile* is a later edition that is a perfect reproduction of the original edition; see *microfiche* and *microfilm*.

An imprint is the printed name of the *publisher* of a book and its date of publication. This information usually appears at the bottom of the title page of the book, and on the verso will appear the notice of copyright, or right of legal publication and reproduction. A pirated edition is one that is illegally published, violating the copyright. Such an edition will generally have a blank verso. The only printed page that precedes the title is the half title, which has the title of the book but not its author. A colophon is an annotation on the last page of some books that gives information regarding the printing, the typeface, the type of paper (see *writing surfaces*), and the designer of the book. The layout is the plan for the format of a book, including its size, shape, binding. Its design includes all of these items.

PROPAGANDA. The methodical dissemination of information or disinformation regarding a *tenet* or cause espoused by a group that wishes to convince an audience of its veracity through *advertisement* and blare rather than discourse. One vehicle of religious propaganda is the *tract*.

PSEUDONYM. A pseudonym, pen name, or nom de plume is a literary alias. An allonym is the real name of a person assumed by an author but not the author's real name. Sometimes an allonym masks a collaboration among several writers. A ghost writer is an author hired by someone to write a text that will be published under the name of the hirer rather than the actual writer. An eponym is the name of a person that has come to be a synonym for some term, as, for instance, "Elizabethan" for the English Renaissance.

PUBLISHING. A trade publisher issues books in a wide variety of categories for general circulation, whereas the alternative press, like the little magazines, caters for a literary, sometimes avant garde audience. The academic press is devoted primarily to scholarly publication, though by the end of the twentieth century a number of these publishers had also invested heavily in literary books, including fiction and poetry. The vanity press publishes books on a subsidized basis, authors paying not only for the printing of their books but also for the overhead of the publisher. Few authors of any note have come out of the vanity press, but A. R. Ammons is an exception, for his first book, *Ommateum*, was a vanity press book. Self-publication, while often frowned on, is not quite the same as vanity publishing, although it is not much more academically respectable; essentially, the author is simply hiring a printer. Many authors, including E. E. Cummings and William Carlos Williams, published their first books this way. Desktop publication is computer self-publishing.

PUFF. See *notes*.

PULP. See *periodicals*.

PURE POETRY. A synonym for lyric poetry; see also *The Book of Forms*.

PURPLE PATCH. See *poetic passage*.

PURPLE PROSE. Overwritten prose. See *poetic passage*.

QUARTER-BINDING. See *bookbinding*.

QUARTO. See *printing*.

QUOTATION, QUOTE. See *journal* and *notes*.

RECENSION. See *collation*.

RECONSTRUCTION. See *manuscript*.

RECTO. See *bookbinding*.

REDACTION. See *condensation*.

REIFICATION. Treating an *abstraction* as a *concretion*; for instance, to approach the subject of deity as though it were tangible is the purpose of divinity, and all "theology" is an act of reification. The term "God" is an abstract noun (see *abstraction*) that is not capable of *conventional definition*, but it has *emotive meaning*: an overtone that carries a weight of approbation with many people, especially those who are religious—see the discussion of cues elsewhere in these pages. It has no cognitive meaning, that is, a meaning that is capable of empirical proof; it cannot be perceived, either with the senses or by means of experimentation. Some critics argue that poetry (at least "*pure poetry*," i.e., lyric poetry, as distinguished from narrative and dramatic poetry) has no cognitive meaning, only emotive meaning, since its purposes are not *ideational* but emotional. See our companion volume, *The Book of Forms: A Handbook of Poetics*.

REQUESTA, RESPUESTA. See *catechism* and *The Book of Forms*.

RÉSUMÉ. See *condensation*.

ROTARY PRESS, ROTOGRAVURE. See *printing*.

RUBRIC. See *chapter heading*.

RUN. See *periodicals* and *printing*.

SCHOLAR. An *academician* or other learned person who is the student of a particular discipline; a loresman.

SCHOLARLY ESSAY. See *document*.

SCHOLIA. See *notes*.

SCHOLIAST. A medieval scholar who annotated the classical authors.

SCRIBE. A copyist. See *documentation*.

SCRIPT. Handwriting; see *manuscript*. A book or text written on a typewriter is a typescript (TS or ts; plural, tss). A carbon copy is a copy of a work made using carbon paper, now generally an obsolete process. A computerscript (CS, cs, css) is a draft of a computer-generated or word-processed hard copy of a work.

Foul copy is a manuscript or typescript that has been used by a printer to set the type for the book. It has been copyedited and contains all sorts of marks intended to instruct the typesetter, and it also contains editorial notes and queries to and from the author and the printer in the margins. A foul proof is a corrected printer's proof that has been submitted to the editor and the author for proofreading before the first printing of the literary work. An uncorrected proof is one that has not yet been marked up. See also *documentation*.

SCRIVENER. A public copyist. See *documentation* and *scribe*.

SCROLL. See *writing surfaces*.

SECONDARY SOURCE. Secondhand information about a subject, such as a contemporary book review of a novel or a collation of published versions of a text. See *documentation* and *microfilm*.

SELF-PUBLICATION. See *publishing*.

SENSABLE. Appealing to the senses, for instance, a concrete *trope*.

SENSES OF INTERPRETATION. There are four senses of interpretation of any literary writing: the *literal* (surface or narrative), the *allegorical* (symbolic), the *tropological* (moral), and the *anagogical* (spiritual), in which allusions to Paradise or the life hereafter are discovered.

SIXTEENMO, 16MO, SIXTY-FOURMO, 64MO. See *printing*.

SIZE. See *printing*.

SLICK. See *periodicals*.

SLIPCASE, SLIPCOVER. See *dust jacket*.

SPINE. See *bookbinding*.

STEMMA. See *variorum*.

STURM UND DRANG ("storm and stress"). An eighteenth-century German literary movement. The term has stuck in a quasi-psychological context to mean the personal turmoil of the author or the author's invented characters, or both.

SUMMARY, SUMMATION. See *condensation*.

SYMBOL. A concrete trope (figure of speech) or a *pictograph* (a picture) that represents an *abstraction* (i.e., in some contexts a great white whale might be symbolic of the insensibility of nature). An emblem is a conventional symbol—a bald eagle is emblematic of the United States of America.

SYNESTHESIA. The trope of talking about one of the senses in terms of another: "Monday morning smells blue" (scent-sight); "I could taste her sweet whispers" (taste-hearing); "He touched me with his mind" (thought-touch). See *symbol*. See also the chapter "The Genres of Nonfiction."

SYNOPSIS. See *condensation*.

TABLE OF CONTENTS. A list of *chapter headings* preceding the *body* of the book.

TACT. The sense of proportion or fitness required when dealing with an audience.

TASTE. See *bibliophilia* and *tautologia*.

TAUTOLOGIA. The overuse of sonic devices, as in a sentence containing too many alliterated words as perhaps in the fourth line of "God's Grandeur" by Gerard Manley Hopkins (1844–89):

> The world is charged with the grandeur of God.
> It will flame out, like shining from shook foil;
> It gathers to a greatness, like the ooze of oil
>
> Crushed. Why do men then now not reck his rod?

Such a style is sometimes castigated as being baroque or artificial, meaning overwrought, like the euphuistic style (see *Euphues* in text), though of course all writing of every kind is artificial in the sense that it is artifice. What critics mean when they use such a word has to do with degree of artifice. The touchstone would no doubt be what seems, to a particular critic, to be too highly wrought, too self-conscious or "literary"; that is, "artsy." In other words, the critic's taste is what is important, at least to the critic if not to the audience the critic is trying to convert to his or her way of thinking. See *The Book of Forms*.

TEXT. See *documentation*.

TEXTE. See *notes*.

TEXTURE. The texture of a work has to do with its style and over-lapping meanings, its sounds, figures of speech, ambiguities; its surfaces and depths.

THIRTY-TWOMO, 32MO. See *printing*.

TOME. A ponderous volume.

TOP-EDGE. See *bookbinding*.

TOUCHSTONE. A line or passage or whole work used as a criterion of excellence.

TRACT. A brief text of some sort, usually a pamphlet or leaflet, focusing on a single topic, generally religious. See *books* and *propaganda*.

TRADE PUBLISHER. See *publishing*.

TREATISE. See *document*.

TREMBLESTICK LEAGUE. See *bardolatry*.

TRIM. See *printing*.

TROPE. A word picture or *figure of speech*. Some tropes are inherently inclusive, for instance, *synesthesia*.

TROPOLOGICAL INTERPRETATION. The moral level of any text. See *senses of interpretation*.

TS, TS, TSS. See *script*.

TWELVEMO, 12MO. See *printing*.

TYPE, TYPEFACE, TYPESETTING. See *printing*.

TYPESCRIPT. See *documentation* and *script*.

UNCORRECTED PROOF. See *script*.

UNCUT, UNOPENED. See *printing*.

VADE MECUM. "It goes with me." Any indispensable book, such as one would take along on a trip or journey or if one were going to be marooned on a desert isle.

VANITY PRESS. See *publishing*.

VARIORUM. An edition comparing several different printings of an author's work according to a stemma (tree of textual descent) or an edition of an author's works annotated by various scholars.

VELLUM. See *writing surfaces*.

VERBATIM TRANSCRIPT. A word-for-word copy of a spoken text.

VERSION. See *secondary source*.

VERSO. See *bookbinding*.

VERTICAL AUDIENCE. See *audience*.

VOLUME. When not simply a synonym for "book," it means one book in a *set* of books or a year's worth of issues in a series of *periodicals* or *magazines* (serials).

WORD PROCESSING. See *script*.

WRITING SURFACES. In the Western world these have included stone, clay, wood, animal skins, and bark. The forerunner of paper—originally manufactured from rags—was papyrus, an ancient thin, flat sheet made from the pith of the Egyptian sedge of the same name; it was rolled into scrolls long before volumes were invented. Before printing, volume manuscripts were written on parchment, the skin of a sheep or a goat prepared as a writing surface, or vellum, a fine parchment made from calf, lamb, or kid. A palimpsest is a writing surface of some kind that that has been used more than one time as material for a *manuscript*.

YEARBOOK. An *annual* publication. See *books*.

Acknowledgments and Bibliography

All material not specifically attributed to another writer, including essays, plays, stories, and translations, is the work and property of Lewis Turco. Some of this matter has previously appeared as essays or portions of essays in various periodicals and texts, to whose editors and publishers the author is indebted for first publication.

Abrams, M. H. *A Glossary of Literary Terms.* 3rd ed., New York: Holt, Rinehart & Winston, 1971.

Baldwin, Charles Sears. *Medieval Rhetoric and Poetic.* Gloucester, Mass., Peter Smith, 1959.

Ball, David. *Backwards and Forwards.* Carbondale: Southern Illinois University Press, 1983.

Barnet, Sylvan, Morton Berman, and William Burto. *A Dictionary of Literary, Dramatic, and Cinematic Terms*, Boston: Little, Brown, 1971.

Colwell, C. Carter. *A Student's Guide to Literature.* New York: Washington Square Press, 1968.

Davie, Donald. *Articulate Energy.* New York, 1958.

Dietrich, R. F., William E. Carpenter, and Kevin Kerraine. *The Art of Drama.* New York: Holt, Rinehart & Winston, 1969.

Eliot, T. S. *The Three Voices of Poetry.* Cambridge: National Book League at the University Press, 1955.

Empson, William. *Seven Types of Ambiguity.* New York: New Directions, 1955.

Field, Syd. *Four Screenplays.* New York: Dell Publishing, 1994.

Grebanier, Bernard. *Playwriting.* New York: Thomas Y. Crowell, 1961.

Greene, David H., ed. *Anthology of Irish Literature.* New York: New York University, 1971.

Groden, Michael, and Martin Kreiswirth, eds. *The Johns Hopkins Guide to Literary Theory and Criticism*. Baltimore: Johns Hopkins University, 1994.

Hall, Lawrence Sargent. *A Grammar of Literary Criticism*. New York: Macmillan, 1965.

Holman, C. Hugh. *A Handbook to Literature*. 3rd ed. Indianapolis: Bobbs-Merrill, 1972.

Horner, Winifred Bryan. *Rhetoric in the Classical Tradition*. New York: St. Martin's, 1988.

Kaiser, Rolf, ed. *Medieval English*. Berlin: Rolf Kaiser, 1961.

Mackay, Charles. *The Lost Beauties of the English Language*. New York: J. W. Bouton, 1874.

Minot, Stephen. *Three Genres.* 3rd ed. Englewood Cliffs, N.J.: Prentice-Hall, 1982.

Pei, Mario, and Frank Gaynor. *A Dictionary of Linguistics.* New York: Philosophical Library, 1954.

Puttenham, George. *The Arte of English Poesie*. Kent, Ohio: Kent State University Press, 1970.

Shaw, Harry. *Concise Dictionary of Literary Terms.* New York: McGraw-Hill, 1972.

Turco, Lewis. *Freshman Composition and Literature*. Albany: State University of New York, 1973.

Waggoner, Hyatt H. *American Poets from the Puritans to the Present*. Boston: Houghton, 1968; rev. ed., Baton Rouge: Louisiana State University Press, 1984.

Warren, Alba H. Jr. *English Poetic Theory, 1825–1865*. New York: Octagon Books, 1976.

Watson, George, *The Discipline of English*. New York: Barnes & Noble, 1979.

Wolf, Jurgen, and Kerry Cox. *Successful Scriptwriting.* Cincinnati: Writer's Digest Books, 1988.

Index

Page numbers in bold indicate glossary entries in the text.

UNIVERSITY PRESS OF NEW ENGLAND publishes books under its own imprint and is the publisher for Brandeis University Press, Dartmouth College, Middlebury College Press, University of New Hampshire, Tufts University, and Wesleyan University Press.

Library of Congress Cataloging-in-Publication Data

Turco, Lewis.

    The book of literary terms : the genres of fiction, drama, nonfiction, literary criticism, and scholarship / Lewis Turco.

        p.   cm.

    Includes bibliographical references and index.

    ISBN 0-87451-954-3 (alk. paper). —ISBN 0-87451-955-1 (pbk. : alk. paper)

    1. Literature—Terminology.   2. English language—Terms and phrases.   3. Literary form—Terminology.   4. Criticism—Terminology. I. Title.

PN44.5.T87   1999

803—dc21

99-23472